SEEING TOMORROW

SEEING TOMORROW

Weighing Financial Risk in Everyday Life

RON S. DEMBO

AND ANDREW FREEMAN

M&S

Canadian Cataloguing in Publication Data

Dembo, R. S. (Ron S.)
Seeing tomorrow : weighing financial risk in everyday life

ISBN 0-7710-2612-9

1. Risk management.   2. Decision-making.
I. Freeman, Andrew, 1963–   .   II. Title.

HD61.D445   1998   658.15'5   C98-930178-8

We acknowledge the financial support of the Government of Canada through the
Book Publishing Industry Development Program for our publishing activities.
We further acknowledge the support of the Canada Council for the Arts and
the Ontario Arts Council for our publishing program.

Typeset in Bembo by M&S, Toronto
Printed and bound in Canada

McClelland & Stewart Inc.
The Canadian Publishers
481 University Avenue
Toronto, Ontario
M5G 2E9

1 2 3 4 5 6   02 01 00 99 98

For Alyson, Justine and Ella

For Hazel

CONTENTS

ACKNOWLEDGEMENTS

This book is the product of a true collaboration. Andrew Freeman met Ron S. Dembo in 1995 when he was researching an article on risk for *The Economist*. He visited the offices of Algorithmics in Toronto expecting to hear typical corporate PR. Instead he was swept into a whirlwind conversation about risk and regret, concepts that had long preoccupied Dr. Dembo and formed the intellectual basis of his software business. Intrigued, the journalist and the academic-turned-entrepreneur debated whether they should try to write something together that described new ideas about the way we all make decisions involving risk. Much cogitating and many late nights ensued. Ideas were swapped by telephone, e-mail, fax, even by traditional letter, as the project grew in scope. The result is *Seeing Tomorrow*.

We must thank many people. Ron Layard-Liesching of Pareto Partners first suggested that we might like each other, adding that we should meet anyway. Over the years plenty of individuals have given generously of their time and ideas in the pursuit of good reporting and sound thinking. Charles Sanford of Bankers Trust and Stephen A. Ross of Yale deserve special mention. Meir Statman of Santa Clara University was especially helpful on behavioural finance. Peter Bernstein, by writing a brilliant book on risk, inspired us to believe that there is widespread interest in the subject. Jacqui Dunal of Algorithmics Inc. was a selfless and enthusiastic contributor to the preparation of a legible manuscript, as well as an essential anchor when the authors were at different ends of the earth. We gratefully acknowledge the help and insights of several others who read the manuscript at an early stage. We remain responsible for any errors that have survived.

The central ideas behind *Seeing Tomorrow* owe much to years of hard work and advocacy by Ron S. Dembo. His ideas on measuring risk, although in print for many years in technical papers, presentations, and a patent, have not been available to the general public until now. Employees at Algorithmics have been invaluable as colleagues and as critics. Special thanks to Michael Zerbs, Michael Durland, Andrew Aziz, Dan Rosen, and David Penny. The many hours spent debating the central ideas with them have contributed to the theory.

Andrew Freeman owes much to his colleagues on *The Economist* and, before that, the *Financial Times*. Special thanks are due to Bill Emmott, the editor of *The Economist*, and to Clive Crook, its deputy editor, for permission to draw on some previously published articles, including a fine and relevant piece on decision theory by Mr. Crook. Merril Stevenson was an inspiring finance editor as well as a wonderful colleague who passed on the art of making complex ideas understandable.

Thanks to our agent, Beverley Slopen, for proving that there can be upside in book writing. Myles Thompson at John Wiley & Sons has been a supportive and enthusiastic editor who needed remarkably little prodding to see the merits of our work. Jonathan Webb at McClelland & Stewart was an insightful and helpful editor of the text.

Thanks to our children, Justine and Ella Dembo and Luke, Max, and Georgia Freeman-Mills, who generously gave up precious time with their fathers so that this book could be written.

Our biggest thanks we offer to our wives, Alyson Hannas and Hazel Mills. They saw at first hand the perils of book writing. They tolerated the daydreams and absences that characterized the progress of ideas into prose. They joked occasionally that the real spouses in this group were the two authors. Without their support, sometimes maintained in trying circumstances, neither of us could have finished this book. Smaller wonder that it is dedicated to them.

Introduction: It Really Happened

Imagine for a moment that you are George Soros, one of the world's best-known investors. You have formed a joint venture with Paul Reichmann, one of the world's best-known property developers. Together you are about to close a huge deal in the hot Mexican economy that will add hundreds of millions to your already substantial fortune. At the last minute, however, there is a hitch. Your prospective local partner wants better terms in order to reflect some turbulence in currency markets – it is late 1994 and the Mexican peso has suddenly fallen and could fall further. Will you agree to change the contract by 10 per cent in your local partner's favour? How should you approach this decision? Do you lock into a sure thing today or wait and hope that things will improve so that your returns are even better? Do you concede or do you play hardball?

Two of the world's shrewdest business brains, George Soros and Paul Reichmann, got this deal completely and horribly wrong. It fell apart and they never did develop a prime site in Mexico City as they had hoped. The full story (see Chapter 1) is an object lesson in how not to make decisions about risk. The deal went wrong because Soros and Reichmann made a classic error in thinking about their decision: they failed to take into account the possibility that things could go from bad to worse. They underestimated the regret that they would feel if the deal failed altogether.

It is not only big players who make such mistakes. Most of us regularly face decisions about risk that can have a huge impact on our lives. Most readers probably know someone who lost everything in the housing market at some point in the last fifteen years. From London to New York and Toronto, house prices have swung up and down with alarming speed. A safe equity cushion one day has become a yawning "negative equity" debt the next. Today's expensive and desirable studio apartment can become tomorrow's unsaleable poky room. Even as this book was in preparation, one of the authors, who sold a house in 1994, watched in dismay as property prices in England defied expectations and rose to new heights. In Chapter 4, we show some telling examples of just how poor our thinking about house-price risk can be.

The truth is that calamities can happen. Sometimes, as in the case of Mexico, the reverberations are felt throughout financial markets and economies. Such events make palpable what we know to be true in theory, that risk lies ahead of us, not behind. It is no use looking over our shoulder and assuming that we will discover there all we need to know either about the stability of a nation's currency or about the constancy of house prices. Yet looking over our shoulder is precisely what most of us do. How many of us have metaphorically kicked ourselves for decisions we got wrong and which seem obvious and easy in retrospect? Chances are that we were guilty of poor thinking, for which read past thinking.

For centuries, mathematicians, economists, and philosophers have sought ways to model how we make choices. Our behaviour is governed by many things – taste, budget, and appetite for risk, to name a few. Financial risk management is based on a number of related calculations. What is our risk exposure? Can we do things that will limit our risk? Are there controls available that will prevent us from suffering excessive loss? It is not just financiers who make these calculations. We all do. For example:

- Should we buy a house now?
- Should we invest in the stock our broker is suggesting?
- Should we pay the seemingly high charge for daily car rental insurance?
- Should we set aside a fund for our three-year-old daughter's college tuition?
- Should we start a pension plan, and, if so, how much should we set aside?
- Should we undergo an experimental medical procedure that might cure us of a longstanding illness?
- Should we refinance our mortgage now or later?
- Should we buy a lottery ticket?
- Should we go on strike and risk losing our job?
- Should we refuse a wage demand and risk a strike that might destroy our business?

We must face and make many of these decisions, and, occasionally, we will regret our choices.

While individuals periodically take risks, financial institutions – banks, brokers, and insurers – do so routinely. They are risk traders. Their business is to profit from risk. In recent years, as financial markets have become dramatically more complex, these institutions have had to develop innovative ways of controlling their risk exposures. But it is inherently difficult for these firms to understand the extent of the risks they are assuming at any given moment. Often their ability to understand risk lags seriously behind their urgent need to do so.

What guides people in making a decision in a financially risky setting? Why do different people place differing amounts on the same bet? Why do some people have larger exposure to mutual funds than others? Why do people change their strategy as the stakes change in a game? How do people measure risk? On what basis do they decide whether to accept a risky bet? Why do they buy lottery tickets or insurance policies even when the odds are against them? How should banks measure and control risk so that the financial system remains healthy?

There are no simple answers to all these questions. Indeed, in our ever more complex world, answering them becomes both more difficult and more consequential. Just think of how much more choice and complexity we encounter compared to our parents. How many options did they have to choose from when mortgaging their house, choosing life insurance, or investing? Mutual funds were scarcely available a generation ago. Nor were such exotic instruments as exchange-traded options. No one had yet dreamed of mortgage-backed securities. It was almost impossible to buy exposure to foreign markets. Today these all exist, and tomorrow the choices will multiply. So what are we to do? It is no longer good enough to operate on intuition alone. We require tools to help us quantify the options we face.

We have written this book because we think it is time to rewrite the rules on risk. Too many mistakes have resulted from outmoded and flawed approaches to defining and managing risk. Perhaps surprisingly, it is a subject that has been largely neglected. It's true that some progress has been made. Huge markets now exist in financial instruments known as derivatives that are designed to lay off or assume risks of various kinds. Individual investors now take for granted information about their investments that was once unavailable or limited to large institutions. But we believe that most of the methods available and in use today are inadequate for analysing the types of risk most of us face.

In some respects, people are far more aware of the problem than they used to be. Masses of consumers have shifted their savings from low-paying bank accounts into money market accounts or more aggressive mutual funds. They have been actively assuming risk in exchange for greater returns. And people purchasing insurance can make much more finely calibrated decisions about how much risk they wish to lay off, although, as we will see, this market remains frustratingly slow at developing useful new policies.

Yet much of this increased awareness and embracing of risk has been accompanied by a giant shrug of the shoulders. Sure, we know we are exposed to more risk, but that's okay, nothing terrible will happen. But many of the everyday ways in which we are exposed to risk are mistakenly overlooked. Moreover, they share common elements with the more formal risk disciplines that are associated with financial markets and banking.

Holding an investment or a portfolio of investments is like taking a gamble. In the end, we will either win or lose. Yet, as we all know, when taking a bet we are often faced with a single, unique decision that will probably not be repeated. We need to make the decision faced with the uncertainty the future brings, and we need to make it now.

We will show that many bankruptcies, bad deals, and large losses come about because most people fail to consider scenarios under which they might lose in a big way. A few people, it is true, adopt a structured approach to decisions that involve risk. They map out their options and assess the pros and cons implied by each one. Many more people tend to act intuitively, however; "go with your gut" is a common approach, and as often as it succeeds it produces horrendous results. It is revealing to analyse some of that intuitive process.

In fact, we lack accepted definitions of risk. We lack agreed ways of measuring risk. In particular, we too often assume that what has happened in the past will be a reliable guide to the future. In the following pages, we will describe a number of concepts that will change all that. Some of these are the result of years of research by Ron Dembo. Through Algorithmics, his software firm, he has shown that apparently abstract ideas can have practical and powerful applications in the real world. Moreover, the framework set out in this book is no different from the one Algorithmics uses to help the world's most sophisticated banks to manage their risk.

The central concept we introduce is that of regret – the neglected "R" behind Risk and Return. As we will see, regret is a common enough idea in several branches of academic economics and finance. But its applicability to risk management has been almost entirely missed. We hope to show that regret is a powerful tool for aligning how we intuitively judge risk with the more formal methods that we use for quantifying it.

But our purpose is far broader and more ambitious than this might suggest. In the following chapters we will show ways of visualizing risk that help to explain the new rules. We also make a few calculations to illustrate how risk measures work in practice. No one should be put off by the formulae involved. They are mostly simple, but even if they prove to be impenetrable for some readers, our main argument should still be clear. Where possible we use words to augment and explain our use of symbols. You should be aware that even mathematicians confess that they, too, sometimes struggle with symbols. Just as cooks must sometimes read a recipe several times before they can relate the instructions to the ingredients that will make the dish, so, too, mathematicians must read and then slowly reread a proof before they can be satisfied that it is correct. For a reader who feels stuck or confused by a passage we have simple advice: don't be afraid to read it again!

None of us can afford to ignore risk – it is always present in our lives. All of us need a better framework for understanding and managing it. We offer the framework described in these pages as a step in the right direction. We think that it captures some aspects of risk that were previously thought to be unquantifiable: we have tried to assess how we as individuals actually think about risk. Our framework is built around our view of the future, not modelled solely on the past. And it is adaptable enough to allow each of us to express our own forward-looking attitudes and fears, rather than relying on the assumption that people have broadly similar views. Unlike some commonly used numerical and statistical measures of risk, it is also closely aligned to our intuitions about how we feel when we eye one risk relative to another. And, finally, we suggest that our approach allows a consistent view of risk. It is coherent whether it relates to a single investment or an entire portfolio. Where other measures of risk break down or are manifestly inadequate, we suggest new and powerful ways of approaching the subject.

People have always been trying to see tomorrow. Raymond DeVoe, a stockbroker who writes a wry newsletter replete with history, points out that the Romans gave us the word "speculator" – it derives from the Latin word *specula*, meaning a watchtower of the kind that ringed the old imperial city of Rome at strategic intervals and from which approaching danger could be spotted. By the apogee of the Roman Empire, the watchtowers stretched for thousands of miles, acting as an early-warning system that allowed the swift dispatch of legions to wherever trouble was brewing. Thus a pure definition of a speculator is someone who tries to see dangers in the future and act upon them. Only more recently did the word "speculator" acquire a pejorative edge in financial markets!

In one fundamental respect, decisions involving financial risk are different from other decisions that we face in life. Whereas many facets of daily life shift with glacial, almost predictable, slowness, financial markets can change in the blink of an eye. Think about it. Let's say you wish to hire a carpenter to build some shelves. In this case, you can be pretty confident that the carpenter who was excellent six months earlier will still be at the top of his trade. In other words, history is an excellent guide. It is unlikely that someone who was very good then will be incompetent now.

Contrast this with finance. A brilliant fund manager can lose everything in a matter of days. Sometimes mere minutes can send a high-flying company's shares into free fall. History is no guide, or at best a guide that can be dangerously misleading. So rapidly can things change that complacency is extremely risky.

In sum, there are times when our intuitions about what is safe are unreliable. A good carpenter does not equate to a good investment. When we buy a share, we cannot relax and assume that we know exactly what we have bought.

As Kenneth Arrow, a Nobel laureate in economics, wrote, "our knowledge of the way things work, in society or in nature, comes trailing clouds of vagueness." We can never know exactly what will happen in the future. But we can try to blow away some of the clouds of vagueness so that we can better understand and manage risk.

1

How to Think About Risk

I t was meant to launch their comeback. When the Reichmanns joined George Soros in a joint venture in Mexico City, it was in the hope of again scaling the financial heights from which they had viewed the world in the 1980s. Their dream was a multi-billion-dollar development in the capital of one of the fastest-growing economies in the world. Mexico appeared poised to break through the barrier dividing developed and developing economies. Its trade links with America and Canada were about to be ratified and liberalized via the North American Free Trade Agreement (NAFTA), which was eventually signed by President Clinton in 1993. But Mexico City had very few modern office buildings and high rents in those that did exist. What could be more appropriate than to revamp a chunk of this sprawling capital city and erect some of the Reichmanns' signature skyscrapers?

In fact, the Reichmann–Soros venture almost succeeded. The Reichmanns followed their typical development process. The venture bought two parcels of land, one of which was on a prime site in the heart of the city. The land was bought on favourable terms from the government on the promise that it would be developed into a top-rate site. By investing a relatively small amount in architects' drawings and marketing, the Reichmanns hoped to lure a local partner into a fifty-fifty joint development venture. A giant publicity fanfare led to lots of interest from big construction firms. ICA, a large local firm, bought a 50 per cent stake in the first parcel of land on the outskirts of city. In bidding for the second parcel, ICA proposed to be the builder as well as joint developer.

It seemed like a sure thing. ICA's cash would fund the entire development, leaving the Reichmanns and Soros with no downside exposure but potentially tremendous upside in the event that the project was a success. A further attraction for the Reichmanns was that they had already dealt with ICA and felt that a deal could be closed quickly.

Unfortunately, the Reichmanns, like much of the rest of the world, were overly convinced that Mexico's American business school-trained leaders knew what they were doing. In 1994, the Mexican economy was under increasing pressure. Although inflation had fallen dramatically from 180 per cent in 1987 to around 8 per cent, growth was sluggish. The Mexican currency was the victim of sudden bouts of nerves among traders that forced the government to intervene heavily in foreign exchange markets. The need to support the currency grew, and Mexico's foreign exchange reserves dwindled from $25 billion in late 1993 to a mere $6 billion a year later. But the interventions kept the exchange rate fairly stable. Few people watching the market had any idea that big trouble was around the corner. If you were looking at the exchange rate to guide, say, an investment such as the Reichmanns', recent history would have given you little idea of what lay ahead.

The key to the peso's relationship to the dollar was a tight band within which the government insisted that it stay. On December 20, 1994, the Mexican government announced that it had widened that band. The peso immediately fell by 10 per cent in a move that shocked traders and investors alike. On December 23, the band was removed altogether and the peso went into free fall against the dollar, losing

50 per cent of its value in the space of a few days. Interest rates quadrupled over the same period. In the months that followed, it became clear that Mexico had suffered a major economic crisis.

How did the Reichmanns and George Soros react? Their deal with ICA was supposed to be signed and sealed on December 20 – the day the peso began to fall. Mysteriously, in the days leading up to the 20th, ICA began to stall. Perhaps the firm sensed that the currency was vulnerable. When the two sides met on December 21, ICA had changed its position. It wanted the 10 per cent fall in the peso to be reflected in new terms for the deal. This was not entirely unreasonable – ICA had to use pesos to fund an investment in dollars that had suddenly become more expensive to buy!

Ironically, the Reichmanns' partner might have thrown a lifeline, if only its right hand had known was the left hand was doing. George Soros's canny hedge fund traders had long since sold their peso holdings, believing the currency to be risky. But Mr. Soros's property arm had no such insight. It carried on as if everything was normal. No warning was sent to the Reichmann–Soros venture, which consequently had little sense of the ugly scenario that was about to unfold.

Assume the deal with ICA was successfully renegotiated. What was the Reichmanns' position? Arguably, because the original deal had been a rich one, the new terms were simply slightly less rich. The Reichmanns still stood to make an extremely favourable deal with great upside. By signing a contract with ICA, they would have ensured that the project went ahead. They would have recovered their sunk costs and they would have been largely insulated from further falls in the peso. In effect, most of the financial risk in the development would have been shouldered by ICA. The best scenario for the Reichmanns was a return of the peso to its former value, which could have added 10 per cent to their upside. The worst scenario was that the peso would continue to fall and the deal could be lost altogether – a large downside.

Paul Reichmann, the family's most influential member, refused to deal. He would not allow any alteration to ICA's terms. Then things happened very fast. As the peso went into free fall after December 23, ICA saw that its timing for the development was lousy – it stood to make insufficient returns in dollars to make the project worthwhile. Not surprisingly, it abruptly lost its appetite. The Reichmanns' come-back was off.

Imagine the scene in Mexico City on December 21. The Reichmanns had to ask themselves whether the initial peso devalua-tion would be the end of the matter, or whether there was more trouble to come. They might have done a simple analysis: what were financial markets telling them about the likelihood of further deval-uations of the peso? A quick look at the currency options markets would have shown that traders indeed expected more bad news. Locking in terms at a 10 per cent lower rate for the peso might turn out to be a bargain if it fell by a further 40 per cent.

But instead the Reichmanns chose a more subjective analysis, per-haps because they were committed to the idea of making a comeback. Or perhaps they looked back at the previous eighteen months of stable U.S./Mexican exchange rates and were lulled into thinking that the 10 per cent drop in rates was an aberration. They concluded that the peso's troubles were temporary and that they should not make any concessions to ICA.

The point is that the Reichmanns bet everything on a single outcome. In effect, they were gambling that a single outlook for the peso would turn out to be correct. In fact, anything could have hap-pened to the peso, so it really made sense to consider several possible outcomes. This is a key point about proper risk management that is often overlooked. When we plan around a single view of the future, we are actually gambling. Sensible planning requires us to consider a multitude of possible events and explore how each one might cause us to react.

We now know that this wrong decision cost the Reichmanns dearly. Those close to Paul Reichmann report that he carried on trying to revive the deal, hoping that things could be ironed out.[*] When it became clear that it would take many months to solve the problems in Mexico, Mr. Reichmann became more reclusive than

---

[*] As this book was going to press, part of the original deal with ICA was, in fact, successfully renegotiated.

ever and showed signs of rapid mood swings. He was clearly suffering from serious regret that he had so badly misjudged the situation.

Even though we may not always be conscious of it, we are all risk managers. As we navigate daily life we must make a host of decisions that more or less explicitly reveal our attitude towards risk. Shall I travel by plane or train? Which detergent has fewer noxious chemicals? Which over-the-counter drug is less harmful? Should I buy a lottery ticket instead of a sandwich? Should I invest in mutual funds, stocks, or bonds? Which securities should I buy and how long should I plan to own them? Should I give up smoking? Our views of risk are surprisingly idiosyncratic – one man's pleasure is another's poison. Hence the diversity of economic and business life.

Hence, too, a rich contemporary debate about the fine line between an acceptable and an unacceptable risk. From nuclear safety to food additives, we are bombarded with often contradictory and confusing information about risks. Is the tiny risk from using the chemical Alar on apples a price worth paying for its otherwise beneficial effects? If consumers had known more about ValuJet's safety record, would the airline have folded before the crash in the Everglades that killed so many travellers? If the American money market funds that invested disastrously in complicated but supposedly yield-boosting derivatives in 1994 had been frank about the risks they were running in order to deliver slightly higher returns, would an investor boycott have forced the fund-management firms to change the funds' approach before an expensive bail-out became necessary? Would people have signed up to be "Names" at the Lloyd's insurance market in London if they had known how much downside risk was involved? Would so many banks have lent money (money they subsequently lost in large amounts) to Robert Maxwell if they had known more about that British tycoon's shaky finances? Why did many of the same banks then take a further bath when they lent another fortune to Eurotunnel, the project to build a tunnel under the English Channel that was as successful in engineering terms as it was hopeless in financial ones? The list of such questions is endless.

It is also daunting, for these broad inquiries point to a central confusion about risk management. At a societal level we rely on governments to maintain or introduce regulations that are designed to protect us from many excessive or unwarranted risks. The ban in some countries on smoking in public is an obvious example, as are rules about handling nuclear waste or processing uranium. Alternatively, institutions such as mutual societies and credit unions have arisen to extend access to risk management to large numbers of people. (Mutual funds achieve the same result by virtue of their transactional efficiency.) In developed economies, these forms of "insurance" have helped to spread financial security and well-being far more widely than was previously the case.

But they have also helped to obscure a central and fundamental aspect of risk: namely, that our attitude towards risk as individuals can often be at odds with that of other people. How we feel about a particular risk depends on our circumstances, not least how rich or poor we are and whether or when we will need to get our hands on hard cash. Our circumstances are unlikely to be precisely the same as everyone else's. Even if two people end up making the same investment decision to, say, buy $1,000 worth of Citicorp stock, it is probable that they will have quite different reasons and motives for doing so. Further, there is a common misperception that risk is purely an active concept, that it only involves accepting the possibility of a negative outcome in the hope of reward. In fact, risk comes in other guises. If we have $1 million, but choose to leave it under the mattress, then we are avoiding many risks. But we are just as certainly assuming others. There is risk in doing nothing, just as there is risk in taking action. Indeed, perhaps the essence of risk management is striking a balance between action and inaction.

From just this preliminary exploration, it should already be clear that risk is a subtle notion. Its meanings and boundaries shift constantly, making it difficult to pin down. An acceptable risk one day might appear a foolish gamble the next. Finding a way of thinking about risk that encompasses this subtlety has eluded generations of thinkers and researchers. Even in this age of high-tech computing, the basic architecture of risk management remains primitive – it is as if all that fancy technology is stored in the intellectual equivalent of a wooden shack.

Much has been written about risk in recent years. Indeed, an unprecedented amount of intellectual firepower has been directed at the subject, not least in the field of finance. So why does risk remain so elusive? One answer is that, for all of our sophistication, we sometimes shy away from asking simple questions, as if this makes it easier to grapple with difficult ones. Plenty of great minds have battled with the meaning of risk, so it seems presumptuous to suggest that we might need to start from first principles. Another answer is more humdrum: rather than seek a comprehensive approach to risk, people have chosen "fit for purpose" solutions. This is the risk-management equivalent of "quick and dirty" computer code. For many business problems, it is a sensible enough approach. But when it comes to investment and financial risks it borders on the cavalier. Why embrace an approach to risk that may be flawed when the outcome could be disastrous? No professional gamblers would adopt such an approach – they know too much about ruin!

In his recent book *Against the Gods*, Peter Bernstein describes how our understanding of risk and risk management has developed over the centuries.[*] Until certain central problems in mathematics and probability theory were solved, our ability to define and manage risk was necessarily limited. Moreover, developments in risk theory have been uneven. For generations little would happen, and then a burst of innovation and activity would drag thinking to a new plateau.

Bernstein asks rhetorically what it is that distinguishes thousands of years of history from what we think of as modern times. After all, that history was chock-full of brilliant individuals whose technological and mathematical achievements were astonishing. The answer, suggests Bernstein, is our acceptance of risk: "the notion that the future is more than a whim of the gods and that men and women are not passive before nature. Until human beings discovered a way across that boundary, the future was either a mirror of the past or the murky domain of oracles and soothsayers who held a monopoly over knowledge of anticipated events."

---

[*] *Against the Gods: The Remarkable Story of Risk* (New York: John Wiley & Sons, 1996)

With helpful scepticism, Bernstein asks whether all the fancy mathematics and computer wizardry of today is dangerously analogous to the graven images and idols before which earlier generations made their genuflections. If we rely too heavily on clever models and "black boxes," might we not be succumbing to a version of the faith that less knowledgeable ancestors placed in deities and shamans? Indeed, therefore, might the false "science" of risk management be a dangerous illusion that itself hides potentially catastrophic risks?

Recent history tends to support this view. Until the dangers of risk management began to emerge during the 1980s, few ordinary people had heard of financial derivatives, for example – those infamous futures and options that supposedly caused a series of corporate blow-ups and disasters in the early 1990s. There are few television-watching households that have escaped at least a passing familiarity with derivatives. In Britain, for instance, the collapse in 1995 of Barings, an august and snobbish bank, led to the equivalent of a countrywide education programme in modern finance.

Similarly, voters in Orange County, California, had an unexpected crash course in finance in 1994 when their investment pool was so severely damaged that the county chose to declare itself bankrupt. How did this disaster happen? Robert Citron, the county's elected treasurer, had recklessly used leverage, hoping to boost returns. In effect, this means taking on risks that are orders of magnitude larger than the underlying stake. He was found out by a big reversal in financial markets.

Some of the biggest and most respectable names in finance and business have fallen afoul of risk management in recent years. Among the best known are Britain's National Westminster Bank, Germany's Metallgesellschaft, America's Gibson Greetings, Merrill Lynch, and Bankers Trust, and Japan's Daiwa Bank, Sumitomo, and IBJ, to name a few. Plenty of other firms have had problems, but have chosen to cover them up rather than to lose face – and public confidence. Many banks, for example, have lost millions of dollars in the process of acquiring trading and operating skills in the notoriously difficult options business.

One big bank was even the silent victim of an audacious robbery, in which clever but criminal staff got inside an options pricing model and used tiny changes to skim off a few million dollars of profits for themselves. They were eventually caught but the bank elected not to prosecute them. It feared (probably correctly in light of other banks' experiences) that the revelation of the swindle would wipe out hundreds of millions of dollars of the bank's overall value as nervous investors decided to place their money elsewhere.

It is impossible to calculate the real cost of risk-management failures among businesses, but it certainly runs to many billions of dollars. In 1995 and 1996 alone, documented losses were some $12 billion. Moreover, there are few signs that firms' reliance on mathematics and machines is diminishing. In the trading rooms that are the temples of modern finance, some of the world's brightest brains are competing to attain, however briefly, the strongest grip on risk. Therein lies competitive advantage – to put it crudely, the ability to wring huge profits from less well-equipped rivals. These are the "model wars," a kind of intellectual and financial arms race that promises fat rewards to the victors.

Should businesses rely less on models and more on common sense? We do not think so, for two main reasons. First, the past few decades have witnessed such rapid developments in finance theory and such rapid growth in the world economy that it is not surprising many firms have occasionally fumbled. The banks that have lost big money in options trades, for instance, have undoubtedly learned painful lessons. The best ones will have made adjustments, grafted new rules and precautions onto older and sloppier systems so that they will not be similarly embarrassed in future. For example, in 1987 Merrill Lynch, arguably the world's biggest investment bank, lost $377 million trading mortgage-backed securities. Since then, having installed new risk systems and maintained a careful watch over its trading, it has experienced no significant mishaps.

Firms like Merrill will also probably have absorbed the lesson that unanticipated problems might pop up somewhere – they can never relax on the job. Occasional losses, sometimes even big ones, are in the nature of life and business. That is why firms set aside money as a cushion – it is known as equity and it is there to fall back on in bad times. That is also why regulators require financial firms to set aside capital. Arguments about how much capital is the right amount to set aside are the main reason for the continuing flourishing of risk management, because those who need the least capital to run the same risks enjoy a profound competitive advantage. What we have seen to date in financial risk management at this level is perhaps best characterized as a series of related lessons about the dangers of innovation. But it is not a sign that there is some fatal flaw in our effort to improve our approach to risk. Indeed, it seems almost self-evident that if the costs of risk management really outweighed the massive benefits brought by a variety of new risk-sharing techniques, then the techniques would quickly have been rejected.

Our second reason for thinking that in machines and mathematics we have not reached a dangerous dead end is that thinking about risk has never been more widespread and has never been conducted at a higher level. What has happened is that the inadequacies of many existing approaches to risk have triggered a flourishing and fundamental debate. The problem is not our reliance on models, but flaws in the models on which we rely.

Arguably for the first time, risk is undergoing a comprehensive dissection, a process that simultaneously informs us in new detail and allows us to adopt and invent new techniques for risk-sharing. Both in our ability to map and understand risk, and in our ability to build mechanisms that allow us to manipulate risk, far from being at a dead end, we are in an era of rich, astonishing, and (thanks to technology) possibly unprecedented progress.

Sharing the Risk

The idea of risk-sharing is an important and often neglected one. As the voters in Orange County found out, a big loss spread among thousands or millions of people causes only moderate or even inconsequential pain for individuals. But where risks are concentrated, the results can be disastrous. Citibank nearly blew itself apart in 1991 because it had made far too many loans to the property industry. It now carefully monitors its lending to try to avoid concentrations that could inflict similar damage. And it can use new financial instruments – credit derivatives, for example – that allow it to lay off to other banks and investors risks that make it uncomfortable.

Or think of an entrepreneur who has a 60 per cent stake in her fast-growing company, but who is overexposed to its fortunes and would be ruined if it failed. She would like to reduce that concentration by investing some of her paper wealth in other assets – modern finance has come up with several ways to help her do just that. By giving up some of the upside potential of her stake to other investors, she can shelter her finances from an extreme negative outcome such as her firm going bust.

Risk-sharing has a long history. Early financiers used the idea as the basis of today's insurance industry. Merchants and traders quickly learned that while they could be ruined individually by the loss of a single ship, if they joined together to form fleets of ships then none of them would suffer unduly because of an occasional wreck. More than a century ago, mutually owned life insurance firms in America and Europe extended the benefits of risk-sharing to the masses, changing millions of people's lives.

Moreover, the desire to manage risk was just as strong among our ancestors as it is today. A random, simple, and intriguing example should suffice. In 1807, a group of middle-class women who lived in Arbois, a small town in the Jura, an area of France that borders Alsace and Switzerland, ran a charitable concern, distributing food and material aid to poor people in the town and its surrounding villages. Of course, they laced their charity with a dose of religion in the form of moral education. But theirs was a lay organization that functioned largely beyond the formal reach of the Catholic Church. And the women displayed considerable acumen in the conduct of their affairs. They sought out the best interest rates for any funds they collected and negotiated fiercely with local contractors to ensure that they were getting value for money when they purchased food.

In the course of their work they travelled extensively throughout the town's environs. And they observed in the fall of 1807 that bad weather, following what had hitherto been a good growing season, had left much of that year's crop rotting in the fields. Instead of wringing their hands, they did something remarkable. They bought a futures contract that would lock in the price of grain that they would pay over the coming winter months. They paid 4 francs per measure for some 200 measures, rather than the then prevailing market price of 3 francs 12 centimes. That way, they knew that their charitable activities could continue in the harsh months when they contributed most in terms of welfare to the community. The fact that, had they been speculating, they would also have locked in a fat profit, probably did not occur to them. Today, the women would probably be running their own investment club and, on the back of their successful trade, would star in their own public television investment show!

Better risk-sharing mechanisms could help people to mute the effects of similar risks on their lives. For instance, if there were a market in housing derivatives (contracts that allowed us to bet on movements in house prices), someone worried about missing out on a big rise in prices could purchase options that would, in effect, pay out compensation to the non-owner. Similarly, owners could buy options that would give them downside protection in the event that the value of their house fell below the carrying cost of their mortgage.

Why don't such markets exist already? There are still plenty of practical barriers standing in their way. For instance, although the property market is closely studied these days, it remains a relatively opaque market in which prices are set rather arbitrarily. There is not yet sufficient reliable and regular price information to allow the development of a meaningful derivatives market, particularly one that would be suitable for individuals. Also, there is no easily defined "standard house" that might be used to allow standardized financial contracts. It is a truism that what one person thinks is a palace is an ugly pile to someone else. Similarly, before there could be a smooth-functioning market in "country risk" there would have to be an agreed definition of economic performance and some means of standardizing how each country measured its output.

It is likely, perhaps inevitable, that such markets will be developed in future, for the power of risk-sharing is compelling. Indeed, the idea of risk-sharing – insurance by another name – is central to our new framework for risk. We are not suggesting that insurance is the same thing as risk, or that of itself insurance is all that is needed for effective risk management. Our framework is more flexible than that. Rather, we want to suggest that if a risk can be understood, then by using modern financial techniques, it should be possible to devise ways of hedging or laying off that risk. And once that is achieved, risk can be managed in two directions: there are some people who will be keen to take on more risk and others who are glad to pay a premium to shed some or all of it. That then forms the basis of a market in which a natural competition between buyers and sellers creates real and transparent prices. Where plenty of risks are traded with transparent prices, it is even possible for individuals and firms to optimize their risk exposures; that is, they can select those exposures, which, for an equivalent level of risk, are likely to produce the highest returns, while selling less efficient assets.

This is not pie-in-the-sky or wishful thinking. In June 1997, for instance, a novel transaction was launched in America that attracted huge interest from investors around the world. Ask most investors if they would like to share the hurricane-damage risk of a big insurer and they would probably balk – all that talk of El Niño might have been a tad unnerving. But consider the following bet that was offered by a leading insurer: you buy a one-year security that yields 11 per cent (well above yields on bonds that carry similar credit ratings); in return, you assume an 80 per cent share of the risk that a single hurricane will cause the insurer losses of more than $1 billion but only up to $1.5 billion. In other words, if the worst happens during a single hurricane season, you will lose all of your principal. Once the insurer has lost more than $1 billion, you will be on the hook for your share of the $400 million maximum exposure. Would you take this bet?

On the face of it, the answer is unclear. So before you decide, you might ask a few questions. How much have past hurricanes cost the insurer, in this case United Services Automobile Association (USAA), a firm which specializes in insuring members of America's military and their families? Hurricane Andrew, the worst storm to hit Florida and the southern coastal states in recent history, cost USAA $555 million of losses in 1992. Fine, but how much would, say, the horrendous

storm of 1926 cost USAA if it happened again today? Using a computer simulation to model that storm's impact, the answer is $800
million – there would be no loss on your stake. So the bet is beginning to look reasonably attractive. Indeed, do some fancier computer
modelling to generate possible storms that could occur in the future
and let the virtual weather rage for 10,000 years and you find that
the likelihood of USAA experiencing a loss greater than $1 billion is
less than 1 per cent. The chance of a loss of more than $1.5 billion
is less than four-tenths of 1 per cent. By now you might be reach-
ing for your chequebook.

That is just what some sixty institutional investors, including banks,
hedge funds, and mutual funds, did. From mid-June 1997 until the end
of that year's hurricane season, they were avid watchers of the Weather
Channel, for while the hurricane season lasted they were exposed to
a unique form of risk. Were USAA to have need, some $313 million of
investors' money was at risk; a further $164 million was tied up in a
second set of securities that carried a lower return but guaranteed the
principal amount for less daring folk. For a deal that started out trying
to raise $150 million, that represented a huge success.

One reason for its success is that the attraction of the securities for
investors went far beyond the probabilities of the single bet they were
offered. Until such deals began to appear – the first widely syndicated
offering was launched in December 1996 for a broad portfolio of risks
underwritten by St. Paul Re, subsidiary of a big insurer based in
Minnesota – investors could only gain exposure to the reinsurance
(that is, the insurance of existing insurance risk) market by buying
the shares of reinsurers. However, that is an inefficient and unreliable
way of capturing reinsurance risk.

The returns from pure reinsurance risks such as those offered in
the USAA deal are highly desirable for investors who are otherwise
limited to financial assets. That is because they are not correlated to
the returns from financial markets. When share and bond prices might
be tumbling, chances are that reinsurance returns will hold up fine.
Adding reinsurance risk to a portfolio should therefore significantly
lower its overall volatility – which, after all, is one of the basic tenets
of modern portfolio theory.

That is a big reason why investment bankers have high hopes for the nascent market in so-called catastrophe insurance bonds and why the rest of us should take note. The technique expands the overall ability of insurers and reinsurers alike to spread risk around. At present, they play a sophisticated game of "pass the parcel" among professionals. But if they can offer pure insurance risks to investors, they can tap vast new demand while avoiding the unnecessary expense of buying cover from their competitors. In time that should make insurance cheaper (because less volatile) and hence more ubiquitous. Insurance risk will, in effect, become a new asset class alongside shares, bonds, and commodities.

There is another impact of catastrophe reinsurance that has perhaps the greatest potential to change financial markets. At present, large industrial firms face an insurance dilemma: it would be too costly to insure every bus, truck, and piece of equipment they own. Consequently, many companies choose to self-insure. Thus, an oil refiner, for example, will assume all of the risk that one of its plants might be destroyed by fire, betting that over time the returns from its other assets will cover the loss more cheaply than if it were to buy continuous coverage. Insurance bonds can change that. A refiner might choose instead to package some of its business risk and offer it as securities to investors. It would, in effect, strip away that risk from its underlying operations. This would in turn affect the risk profile of its other issued securities. (By implication, the price of its shares should rise.) In essence, the financial technology that creates reinsurance bonds can be used to develop a class of risk that was previously undiversifiable. Provided the risks are carefully defined and can be priced to attract investors, there should be no lack of demand for such bonds.

Anyone who can understand these related ideas is well on the way to grasping the essence of modern finance, even if they have never used the arcane language of derivatives and portfolio theory. In the chapters that follow, we will explore these ideas in more detail. But our next step is backwards. Before we explain a new framework for managing risk, we need to lay out the basic building blocks of risk and risk management – the pieces we need if we are to understand and control risk.

2

THE ELEMENTS OF RISK MANAGEMENT

A few simple ideas about risk and how we can manage it are sufficient to unlock many otherwise impenetrable questions. For instance, at the most basic level, why are we motivated even to define and to manage risk? The answer is that we worry about what might happen in the future. We know that we are likely to have an array of experiences, some pleasurable, some painful, some potentially fatal. At the very least, we are strongly motivated to avoid or minimize our exposure to the latter. For investors, this means avoiding relative as well as outright financial losses.

Most existing risk-management theory has tended to evaluate risk by looking at what happened in the past. That idea – the extrapolation of the past into the future – is not an entirely stupid one if it is used with care. But very often, as they would reluctantly admit, both large institutions and individuals alike adopt this flawed concept (or variations upon it) as the main basis for their management of risk.

And that, whether from the viewpoint of managers whose jobs depend upon success or of shareholders whose money is at stake, is decidedly scary.

Only a few central elements are required to create a risk-management architecture that is as robust as it is flexible. Our starting point is a definition of risk: *risk is a measure of the potential changes in value that will be experienced in a portfolio as a result of differences in the environment between now and some future point in time.* This definition clearly covers financial risk – the idea, for example, that we might own a share that falls in value over the coming year. But by incorporating the notion of a portfolio, we think we have also covered more general forms of risk. Everyone owns a portfolio whether or not we think of it as such. Thus, our portfolio of risks includes the possibility that we will crash our car or win the lottery, as well as financial assets such as mutual funds.

With this definition in mind, we can examine the main elements required for forward-looking risk management.

- Time Horizon: over what period of time are we concerned to consider our exposure to risk?
- Scenarios: what events could unfold in the future and how would they affect the value of our investments?
- Risk Measure: what is the unit we are using to gauge our exposure to risk?
- Benchmarks: what are the points of comparison against which we can measure our performance?

Let's examine these elements one by one.

The first thing we need to know is our *time horizon*. Over what period of time are we hoping to manage risk? If we think just about the risk of investing money and losing some of it, someone retiring next week will have a very different time horizon from someone just starting work. A soon-to-be pensioner might recoil in horror from an investment that has a big risk of losing money in return for a big payoff, but which will be over in a few days. The potential gain is not worth the risk of losing money that soon will be needed to provide a regular monthly income. By contrast, a new worker might readily embrace the same investment, on the assumption that a loss in the next few days can be overcome by superior returns in the years that will follow.

This was clearly demonstrated on October 27, 1997, when the New York stock market suffered its biggest ever one-day fall. Commentators on that evening's news broadcast were almost unanimous in pointing out that the only people who should really worry about the collapse were those close to retirement. All other investors were reminded that they were in stocks for the long haul. It is important to recognize that our own time horizon should change in line with our circumstances. Thus, that new worker might alter his time horizon to reflect events in his life. Marriage and children, with their associated costs, can entirely shift the length of time over which a person wishes to view the future.

Even this simple idea hides complexities. Not only will most people adopt more than one time horizon in the course of their lives, but they may also have multiple horizons at a given moment. They might have some assets to which they attribute a very long horizon – a young worker's retirement fund, for instance. (In the extreme case, some young workers might choose not to have a retirement fund – their time horizon simply does not stretch that far.) Other assets will be treated with much greater immediacy. And of course, by implication, our time horizons help to determine how we feel about different aspects of our overall exposure.

We can easily make mistakes if we fail to think carefully about the time element of risk. Imagine that we take on a substantial mortgage in order to buy a big but dilapidated house with the intention of fixing it up. We stretch our finances as far as we can because we love the long-term potential of the renovated property. But then interest rates rise by 2 per cent, pushing up the cost of our mortgage. Suddenly our time horizon has shrunk dramatically. We no longer think about choosing paint colours for the long term. Instead we are worried about how to survive financially today. The idea that we can afford to renovate the house has simply retreated until better times return.

In the 1920s and 1940s, economists such as Frank Knight and George Shackle learned to distinguish between risk and uncertainty, using the former term to embrace what can be quantified with certainty, and the latter term to describe our inability to know for sure what will happen. When we choose a time horizon, we are implicitly choosing a period over which we wish to describe the uncertainty of what lies ahead.

Imagined Futures

Our second requirement for risk management is to develop *scenarios* that describe what could happen in future. What is a scenario? In essence, it is a series of linked observations about the state of the world at some predetermined future time. To understand the concept better, let's look at how George Shackle grandly and brilliantly described a decision: "Decision . . . is the imagining of rival paths of affairs; the assigning of these paths to the respective actions, amongst those the decision maker can envisage, which seem to make them possible; and the resolving upon that action which, at best, offers a sequel more powerfully out-weighing what it threatens at worse, than any rival action." In other words, whether consciously or intuitively, we use scenarios ("rival paths") when we make decisions. We use them to imagine what might happen in the future, good and bad. And we include in them everything we think is relevant to us, or at least everything that it occurs to us might be relevant – there is always a scenario that includes something we had not thought of!

Scenarios are part of everyday life. Politicians deal in scenarios as a stock in trade. Think of the phrase "a heartbeat away from the presidency." It puts into words the scenario in which a vice-president of the United States steps into the top job because the president drops dead. Media and academic pundits who monitor election trends make a living by spinning scenarios – what if the Conservatives win 250 seats, and so on. In Canada's ongoing debate over the constitutional status of Quebec a variety of scenarios have been explored. For example, if that province achieves independence, investors based outside the country will likely revise their attitude towards the riskiness of Canada. Banks in Canada are known to hedge (in effect, to protect themselves by buying insurance) against extreme interest-rate volatility each time the constitutional question is revisited. Similarly, debate in Britain about constitutional reforms such as the devolution of Scotland and Wales requires speculation about how power might be divided in future. What will happen to the Labour government's huge majority under different scenarios, and what will happen to Britain's tax system if large parts of the country become semi-autonomous? Equally, what are the implications under different policies of Britain's putative membership in the European Monetary Union?

Another big user of scenarios is the military. The high command of various nations routinely models the different scenarios that might determine the outcome of, say, a combined land-sea attack. What if the weather is cloudy? Could there be a sandstorm that will reduce the mobility of ground units? What would happen to projected casualty rates if the enemy has 10 per cent more troops than reported by reconnaissance units? Military commanders also use scenarios in sophisticated computer models and programs that simulate combat situations. These are much more than fancy video games. At a high-tech research laboratory in Malibu, California, field officers model combat using a simulator that sets a scenario and then plays out battles. Commanders can assess the field and then deploy their troops as they see fit. The modellers learn from the outcomes how the best soldiers make effective choices. By building such "captured knowledge" into regular training for all officers, the performance of real soldiers should improve, resulting in fewer casualties. Similarly, many pilots these days are trained "virtually" – instead of flying a real airplane, they learn on sophisticated flight simulators that can be programmed with different scenarios.

Scenarios give us a basis for evaluating how we might feel about different possible outcomes, which in turn will shape how we will make decisions. This is another area where our individual feelings play a role. As investors, for instance, clearly we all face the same sets of possible outcomes. But our willingness to accept some outcomes as opposed to others varies, just as our time horizons vary. And individually we will probably attach quite different weights to the variables that we use when we model our scenarios.

How we feel about that scenario will depend upon how likely we think it is to occur. In the real world, if we were to embrace a single

scenario we would be putting all our eggs in one basket. We would
not be managing risk, but rather counting on a single outcome. In
effect, we would be forecasting as if we knew with certainty what
was about to happen. Surely no one is so silly? On the contrary. Entire
businesses have been brought to their knees by "single-scenario forecasting." Nor have individuals been infallible. Think of those people
whose fingers have been badly burned because they assumed that
house or mutual fund prices would always rise.

If we are to understand and use scenarios properly, we will generally need lots of them to take into account a wide range of possibilities from that which is most keenly desired to the most disastrous.
Even if we accord it only a very small weight, reflecting the fact that
it is extremely unlikely to occur, our very acknowledgement of nasty
scenarios will alert us to otherwise hidden risks.

Scenarios, then, are powerful tools for reducing the uncertainty we
face when we look forward. Some scenarios, particularly short-term
ones, can reasonably be based upon historical precedent. If a share
is priced at $10, typically moves by around 50 cents, and has never
moved by more than $2 up or down in a single trading day, a one-day
scenario in which the price is essentially stable may be realistic. Other
scenarios, however, are useful precisely because they include the possibility of a sudden change that overturns all our assumptions. What
if the one day we care about turns out to be the day when our share
price tumbles to $4 because the firm announced terrible earnings?

Scenarios do not solve everything, but they represent a big improvement on the forecasting that is so prevalent in business and ordinary
life. Clearly, if we were asked to forecast the value of a bond portfolio
in one year's time we would have to admit defeat – we simply do not
know the answer. But it is relatively easy to come up with a set of scenarios that captures likely and extreme values for the portfolio.

Without scenarios on the future, it is impossible to develop a
coherent framework for risk management. The force of this point
can be neatly demonstrated by a series of questions. Assume for a
moment that we are running a company, which has a portfolio of
businesses (it could just as well be an investment portfolio contain-
ing a combination of assets). What do we think will happen? We

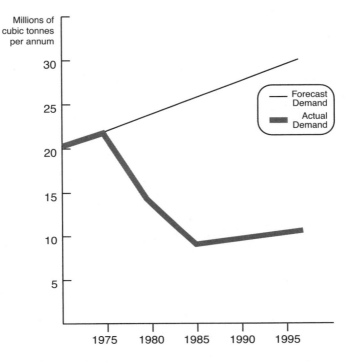

Figure 2.1. To build or not to build? This graph shows how planners usually make a forecast. The broad line shows the actual shipping tonnage required in the period from 1975 to 1995. The narrow line shows what an industry forecaster predicted would be required in the same period based on demand in the preceding period. Single-scenario planning of this kind is dangerous: such forecasts rarely match actual outcomes.

have selected our portfolio of businesses because we think they stand a good chance of generating returns that we can use to pay staff and leave a profit on the table. But is it possible that our judgement is wrong? Might we have made a poor selection that will go horribly wrong and force us into bankruptcy? That is certainly possible, even though we think it unlikely. By implication, we agree that there is more than one possible outcome – we could do fine or badly. Logically, there is a third possible outcome: we could do okay, just well enough to break even. In fact, there is an infinite number of possible outcomes. We cannot adequately manage our risks unless we somehow take them all into account. We cannot review all possible

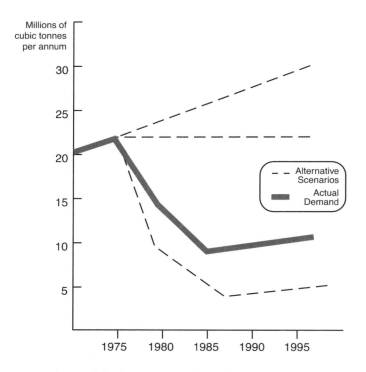

Figure 2.2. A forward–looking approach to planning. If, *instead of relying on a single-scenario forecast, shipping industry planners had considered a variety of scenarios, they would have been in a much better position to deal with adverse outcomes. This graph shows how alternate forecasts of demand bracket actual demand. A key to constructing scenarios is to consider extremes in either direction.*

scenarios, but we can certainly pay attention to those scenarios that we most want to avoid.

Kees van der Heijden, a professor at Strathclyde University in Britain, has described the role scenarios can play in a firm's strategic planning. He worked for years at Royal Dutch/Shell, an international oil group that has been a pioneer of scenario planning. And he clearly shows how fallible businesses can be unless they accept the limits of forecasting.

Every four years over a twenty-year period the Association of West European Shipbuilders published forecasts of demand for world shipbuilding. The forecasts were consistently in error because planners assumed that recent trends would continue. For someone

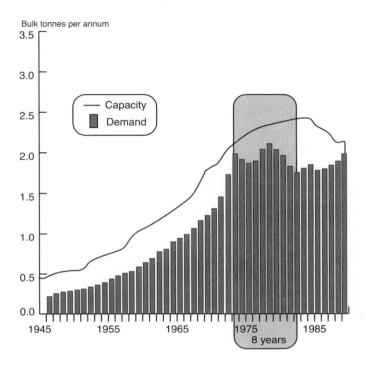

Figure 2.3. World oil demand and refining capacity. *This graph shows how oil industry capacity (represented by the black line) continued to rise even as demand (represented by vertical bars) for oil fell following the 1973 oil crisis and, again, later in the 1970s and 1980s. Firms were slow to react to altered circumstances. Once again, their principal mistake was to make decisions based on a single-scenario forecast.*
Source: Kees van der Heijden, Scenarios: The Art of Strategic Conversation *(New York: John Wiley & Sons, 1996)*

running a shipyard, these supposedly helpful forecasts were actually worse than useless. They were positively dangerous, because they gave the impression of certainty where none existed.

Van der Heijden has also examined the impact of the 1973 oil crisis. Since the end of the Second World War, oil companies had been used to steady growth in demand. There was little focus on strategic planning because 6 or 7 per cent annual growth was seen as reliable. Oil firms simply added new capacity and assumed that growing demand would make it economic. When the oil crisis hit (see figure 2.3), firms continued to pile on capacity as if nothing had happened. It took the industry two years before the growth in capacity slowed down, and another five or six years before the industry significantly altered its behaviour. That lag can be measured in billions of dollars of wasted construction and price pressure caused by overcapacity.

There was a similar delay before oil firms began ordering fewer tankers. Once they woke up, there was a dramatic drop in demand for tankers while the overcapacity that had built up worked its way through the system. Many readers might remember pictures from the late 1970s of hundreds of idle and empty tankers stranded in anchorages around the world, while many in the shipping industry will recall the disastrous effect the overcapacity had on freight shipping rates.

Van der Heijden then asks: what if, by using scenarios, a firm had been able to adjust its business to suit conditions in the space of a single year rather than three or four? Think of the ensuing competitive advantage. What if more firms were prepared to think the unthinkable? Imagine sitting in a strategy meeting at IBM in 1980. You are discussing the future market for the personal computer. The market forecast is that there will be 275,000 machines in use in a decade's time, so it seems obvious that IBM should outsource the machine's operating system and chips. Now, suggests van der Heijden, suppose an outsider walks into the room and announces that the market for PCs will be 60 million, and warns of the dangers inherent in becoming dependent on suppliers like Microsoft and Intel. That person would probably have been laughed at. But the example illustrates the potential of scenarios to change how we think. If IBM had considered a possibility that seemed remote in 1980, it might at least have hedged its bets. Tougher contracts with Microsoft and Intel would have been cheap protection from a worst-case scenario.

Measuring Up

The next thing we need for risk management is a *risk measure*. We need a unit to gauge riskiness. This may seem basic but, surprisingly, measurement of risk is one of the biggest challenges in finance.

We have already observed that traditional risk management has tended to impose broad measures across the board, rather than (correctly) tailoring measures to specific risk appetites. It is widely accepted among financial managers that such broad risk assessments can have dangerously limited application. A simple example comes from the technique known as "value-at-risk" (VaR). This measure is used to describe how much money ("value") is at risk in a firm or bank over a given period at a given moment. Although it appears to reduce risk to an easy-to-understand number, it can disguise or overlook terrifying risks by virtue of its simplifications. And it offers managers little guidance as to where risks are lurking in their organization. For example, two trading desks might generate exactly the same number for value-at-risk, even though the Russian bond-trading desk is clearly riskier than the French equities desk. Almost all risk measures quoted to us are backward-looking. To be useful, a risk measure must take extreme possibilities into account, perhaps including possibilities that have either never occurred or occurred only in the distant past.

In addition, there has been a widespread tendency to separate how we measure risk from how we make investment decisions. In other words, we have suffered from a disconnection between the units we use to account for risk and the metric we apply when we allocate our economic and financial resources. In a comprehensive risk framework, these should be closely related.

The idea of risk measurement is linked to another poorly understood area of risk management: our need for a *benchmark*. We need to be able to make comparisons. Without a point of comparison, we have no idea how one experience has turned out relative to another.

Benchmarks are like scenarios in that we are always using them, even if unconsciously. When we buy something, we usually look at alternatives and ask ourselves whether we are getting the best deal. Someone may have told us about the bargain they got on something and that price becomes our benchmark when we go shopping for the same item ourselves. We are always making comparisons that involve a benchmark. If we feel dissatisfied because our friends all live in bigger houses than we do and drive fancier cars, then our dissatisfaction stems from the perception that we are underperforming the benchmark of material comfort they have set. If four colleagues are promoted while we are passed over, then we will feel that we are underperforming the benchmark of corporate success. Of course, in both cases, we should ask whether these benchmarks are right for us. We might live in a smallish house and drive an old wreck, but if we drink fine wine every day and take expensive vacations, then we may be performing admirably in relation to an alternative benchmark.

The idea of benchmarks has not escaped modern finance. Indeed, the industry is littered with benchmarks designed to describe how markets and groups of instruments have performed. Think of the intense competition between, say, the Dow Jones Industrial Average and the Standard & Poor's 500, not to mention the Russell 2000 index, to be the best measure of the health of the American stock market. But an important aspect of a helpful benchmark has been largely overlooked. Remember the observation that we all have our own attitude towards risk? It follows that, rather than taking measurements from some arbitrarily chosen market average, we should all have our own benchmark, one that is appropriate to our view of the world. A benchmark should be designed to reflect both the context of its user and the context in which it is being used. Further, we need to grasp that a benchmark is not a static thing. Just as the results of our actions depend on the scenarios that unfold, so our benchmark, if it has been properly chosen, is affected by the same factors that define those scenarios. In other words, and counter-intuitively, a benchmark is a fluid concept. At different times and reflecting changing circumstances, we might choose one benchmark in favour of another.

These four elements – time horizon, scenarios, risk measure, and benchmarks – are the essential building blocks of forward-looking risk management. With these elements in place we can begin to do some remarkable things. Once we have a sound basis for comparing the relative riskiness of things, we can accurately measure risk-adjusted valuation. If we know how much risk we have taken for a given level of performance, then we can determine whether we have been adequately rewarded, or, to put it another way, we can give true expression to our appetite for risk. Risk-adjusted valuation gives us a tool to help us decide one way or another when we look ahead at an uncertain future.

A helpful way to understand this concept is to think in terms of self-insurance. Because, as Peter Bernstein put it, we are "against the gods," when we face a risky deal, we need insurance. The chances are that sometimes our calculations will go awry and we need a cushion to catch us. If we don't buy insurance, then we are self-insuring. Implicitly, we are indicating that we have sufficient money to cover the loss. If we choose to insure, then we will often adopt an element of self-insurance by choosing a deductible. To reach a risk-adjusted valuation in this situation, we should price into deals the cost of insurance, whether we self-insure or actually buy protection. In other words, proper valuation takes into account the cost of our potential losses. Imagine we want to buy a $20,000 diamond ring. If we were to lose the ring, the replacement cost might well be beyond our means. We cannot afford to self-insure. So we need to factor into our purchase the annual insurance premium that will protect us against loss. That will give us a risk-adjusted price for the ring. In some cases we will be forced to decide that we cannot afford the ring, even though we have saved the $20,000 ticket price. By contrast, if we buy a $100 child's bicycle, then we might happily self-insure. In this case, the replacement cost is small, so the deal remains affordable even after that cost is reflected in the price. Risk-adjusted valuation is best understood in this context as a form of mental accounting for the replacement cost in the event of loss.

Risk-adjusted measures are powerful tools. They have the potential to change the way millions of people behave and the choices they make. One should never make a decision or take an action based on absolute prices or returns. Indeed, a principal purpose of this book is to encourage people to think in terms of risk-adjusted measures.

Finally, we need a measure that allows us to compare the risk / reward characteristics of two alternative outcomes. Only with such a measure can investors make informed trade-offs when they, say, choose between two mutual funds. Such a measure is entirely absent from most investment choices today. We suggest how a measure might be

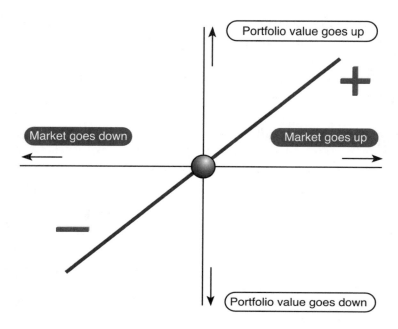

Figure 2.4. A simple view of risk. *The centre point represents the portfolio we hold today. The black line represents our exposure to future changes in value. These could be either up or down.*

formulated and then applied to help people balance their fear of losing money and their desire to make it. This approach allows them to produce the range of exposures that has the greatest risk-taking efficiency. In effect, they can optimize their risk-taking.

This risk architecture is rich in complexity and subtlety. Before we explain how it works in practice, however, we need to introduce some ways of visualizing risk.

In different ways and to different degrees all of us are constantly exposed to possible outcomes, good and bad. The simplest way to see our overall exposure is as an array of positions on a two-dimensional chart (see figure 2.4). The "thing" represented could be something as complex as our entire finances, or as relatively simple as a small port-folio of investments. In the latter case, the portfolio has the potential either to rise or fall in value, but it is made up of a mixture of smaller positions, some of which might indeed rise while others fall. The

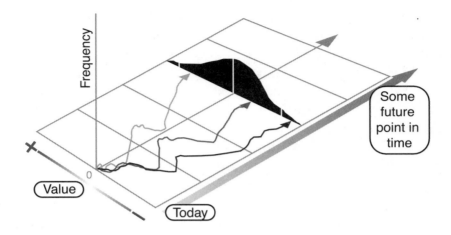

Figure 2.5. Risk in future. *Viewed from today (the point indicated by 0 on the graph), our portfolio may be worth either more or less than its current value. The likelihood of a particular value being achieved is indicated by the curve — whether it is weighted more to the positive or negative side of the central axis.*

two-dimensional snapshot view shows this mix of upside and downside potential outcomes. When we own a portfolio and are exposed to all of those outcomes, our net gain or loss will be the sum of the outcomes. In the language of finance, we have a "long" position in the portfolio.

A richer view of risk is provided by a slightly more complex chart (see figure 2.5). Imagine that we take our simple view and lay it out somewhat differently. The value of our portfolio at the present moment is represented by the point 0. On either side of it are negative and positive values — we know that we could make or lose money as we move forward in time. The value of our portfolio will be affected by many different variables: interest rates, exchange rates, growth rates, yields, and so on. The jagged lines each represent possible future scenarios and the impact on our portfolio of our market variables.

Identifying and mapping these risk variables is a key part of risk management. Unfortunately, however, it is also difficult. Remember that what we are doing is creating a model of the world by abstracting from reality. The world is extremely complex; we cannot hope to model it in all its diversity and unexpectedness. Even for a simple portfolio there might be dozens of risk variables. For a complicated one, or for a simulation of a family's overall exposures, there could be a million variables. From a mathematical point of view, to cope even with a dozen variables requires great skill and computational muscle. To do the job properly, we have to know how each variable affects the others and then how to take that into account. The trick in risk management is to identify the most important variables — the ten or so that will account for 90 per cent of the result. In effect, we need to exclude as many of the meaningless elements of the variable set as we can confidently identify. An American investor, for instance, might choose to exclude Bulgarian interest rates (although a Bulgarian investor might not feel the same way about U.S. rates). Similarly, an investor who only invests in assets denominated in her home currency might ignore exchange rates (although this con-strained approach to investing might not produce the best risk-adjusted returns).

There are many potential values depending upon what happens. For risk-management purposes, we need to select those potential values that are of greatest consequence for us. That is where our time horizon comes in. Let's say that each line on the grid represents three months. In this case, our time horizon is nine months. Using scenar-ios that alter the balance of the variables we have chosen, and weight-ing each scenario to reflect how likely we think it is, we can calculate the different outcomes for our portfolio. Each set of scenarios will produce a different result. In this case, we have shown how three out-comes will produce more or less return over nine months. Figure 2.5 shows a different way of viewing the future using three scenarios, but one which makes explicit that outcomes can be negative as well as positive. If we calculate lots of these results then we can begin to array them from best to worse. That ranking, in effect, produces a line showing how our future outcomes are distributed. Visually it is easy to see how that distribution is weighted — if it "bulges" to the left, then there are more positive outcomes than negative ones, and vice versa. In the example we show (see figure 2.5), the distribution is

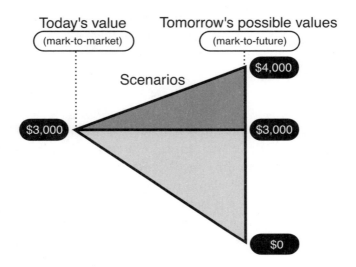

Figure 2.6. Marking-to-future. In this example, the value of your portfolio today is $3,000. If you choose to enter into this deal, there is a chance that it may increase in value to $4,000 over the given period. There is also a chance that it will decrease to $0. Therefore, your decision has an upside of $1,000 and a possible regret of $3,000.

quite even and close to what mathematicians and statisticians refer to as a "bell-shaped" curve. But remember the stress we have laid on always including scenarios that will produce some negative outcomes? Any curve that bulged only to the left of today's value might look like an attractive bet – indeed, it would appear close to a sure thing. In fact, it might be an extremely risky bet because the scenarios have been skewed towards the positive.

So, very easily we have constructed quite a complex picture of risk. It has several dimensions. It is forward-looking, so it helps us to keep in mind the most important risk-management questions. It uses scenarios that incorporate the key risk variables that will affect our future over a specified time horizon. And it neatly shows us how our portfolio will react under different scenarios.

The elements that are combined to form this new paradigm for measuring risk now include upside and downside, present value (mark-to-market), possible future values (mark-to-future), and benchmarks.* A benchmark, in this context, is simply another port-folio, typically with the same market-to-market value today, but pos-sibly different values in the future. The benchmark is essential to provide a baseline against which possible outcomes can be compared.

These elements are shown in figure 2.6 where three different sce-narios are represented by diverging lines leading to more or less favourable results. Each line may be said to form the branch of a tree connecting today's value with possible future values. These futures could be said to refer to the "aged" portfolio, that is, the portfolio as it would appear after the elapse of a specified period of time. The scenario indicated by each branch of the tree can be accorded a weight or probability that reflects how likely we think it is to occur in relation to other possibilities. The range of scenarios may become quite complex, but even in a very complicated tree, the sum of the probabilities will always equal 100 per cent. Trees feature in some key chapters of this book, so it is important to understand what they rep-resent. Let us see how they can advance our thinking about risk.

*"Marking-to-future" is a new concept developed by one of the authors. For a more detailed explanation, see Ron S. Dembo, "Marking to Future," in Carol Alexander (ed.), *A Handbook of Risk Management* (New York: John Wiley & Sons, 1998).

3

OF DECISIONS AND RISK

F inancial risk is measured in a number of ways. Many of these measures are based on probability. It might be said, for example, that there is an 80 per cent chance that you will earn a 7 per cent return, but a 20 per cent chance that you will lose one-third of your investment. Yet most of the decisions we take are one-off – we face them on a single occasion. For these decisions, probability is not necessarily an appropriate guide. It measures the average over a very long run of the same bet. If we are asked to buy a lottery ticket, then we will naturally want to know the probability of winning. But the chances are we won't analyse the lottery on this basis. More to the point, we won't have the luxury of being able to play the lottery over and over again until our final result approximates what the probability measure is telling us.

What we need, then, is a way to analyse one-off situations. In a recent lecture, Peter Bernstein noted that there is a persistent tension between the probabilities that are based on measurement and the

probabilities that come from the gut: "what do we do when the probability of one outcome is much greater than the probability of another
outcome, but the consequences of being wrong are much greater for
the outcome with the lower probability?" In the end, those consequences must dominate the probabilities.

Economists have long known that we mainly tend to face one-off
decisions. But much formal economics assumes the opposite. This has
led to some memorable outbursts. In 1958, for instance, George
Shackle made a trenchant case: "To most businesses it falls only once
or twice, or a handful of times, to have to decide upon the purpose,
type, scale and location of an individual plant; most professional men
choose a career only once; and so on. These occasions of choosing are
spread at such long and irregular intervals that they cannot be treated
as together forming a seriable experiment." He went on: "What is the
sense of a weighted average that adds together a hundred falsehoods
and one truth after multiplying each by some irrelevant number?"
This represents perhaps the strongest objection to probability-based
decision-making.

How we think about the choices that we face can usually be couched
in terms of risk. What is the risk of doing A versus B or C? The answer
is clearly relative. How will we feel if we choose one course over
another, particularly if it turns out after the event that we have made a
bad choice? How do we relate our knowledge of each option's absolute
risk to our own circumstances and consequent tolerance for risk?

The answers to these questions are difficult partly because our
intellectual understanding of risk is less advanced than our intuitive
sense of it. Thanks to its complex nature, it is difficult for us to model
risk in ways that are useful in the real world. Indeed, our typical mathematical descriptions of risk (for which Nobel prizes have been
awarded) can prove dangerous if they are applied religiously in the
real world. This is best illustrated by a simple example.

In your hand you have $10. You must decide which of two mutual
funds to invest your money in for one month. Because each fund
holds different assets, there is a different set of outcomes in the event
that market circumstances change over the course of the month. For
example, should interest rates stay the same, move up, or move down,

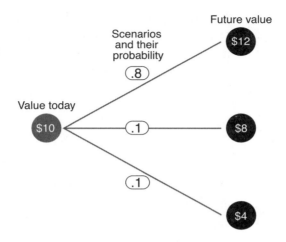

Figure 3.1. Mark-to-future for Fund A. *The initial stake, $10, is to be invested for one month. Thanks to possible events, such as movements in interest rates, there is an 80 per cent chance that the stake will rise to $12; a 10 per cent chance that it will fall to $8; and a 10 per cent chance that it will fall to $4.*

then there will be different effects on the funds. Assigned a probability, each possible event will have an effect on the investment outcome that you know in advance. This is where our tree pictures of risk come in handy.

Figure 3.1 shows the mark-to-future for Fund A.

There are a number of different ways to analyse the risks of this proposed investment. There is a 20 per cent (that is, 1-in-5) chance that you will lose money. But the chances are 80 per cent (4 in 5) that you will gain something. You can be 90 per cent confident that you will lose no more than $6 of your original $10.

This approach focuses on how much of your present value you have "at risk" (hence it is known as value-at-risk [VaR]). This measure of risk has become a standard by which banks and other financial firms try to measure their exposure to potential losses. It has even been sanctioned by international regulators as a sensible way for firms to measure risk. (See Chapter 5 for a longer discussion of VaR.)

In this case of Fund A, you know that your absolute VaR is $6.

Another approach to risk takes into account the fact that over time there is some average outcome arising from the three possibilities. Look again at your three possible outcomes in Fund A ($12, $8, $4) and then weight them by the likelihood that they will occur. You know that these weights are 80 per cent, 10 per cent, and 10 per cent respectively. The sum is as follows:

$$\$12 \times 0.8 + \$8 \times 0.1 + \$4 \times 0.1 = \$10.80$$

That is, the average of these outcomes is $10.80. In other words, assuming nothing changes in your range of possible interest-rate movements, over time and by the law of averages you stand to increase your $10 stake by 80 cents each month. You also know that some months, thanks to adverse movements, you will lose money. But on average the outcome of investing in this mutual fund will be positive.

What if you are worried not about the average outcome, but about a more subtle question − how much potential outcomes will vary around the average? This is known as the "variability" of the outcomes around the average (often referred to as "variance"). It is calculated as follows:

$$0.8 \times (12 - 10.8)^2 + 0.1 \times (8 - 10.8)^2 + 0.1 \times (4 - 10.8)^2 = 6.55$$

A further common measure of risk is known as "volatility" − it is the square root of variance, in this case = 2.56

Some investors think that an investment that has a high variance or volatility is inherently risky. The reality is more complicated. For instance, it is intuitively obvious that Fund A offers you a good chance of an outcome that will be above average − any variability in this fund is skewed in the investor's favour.

So, to recapitulate, Fund A has a VaR of $6, a variance of 6.55, and a volatility of 2.56.

Now consider a second mutual fund that has slightly different characteristics. Given the same initial $10 stake, it will react differently to the same events (i.e., changes, or otherwise, in interest rates) as shown in figure 3.2.

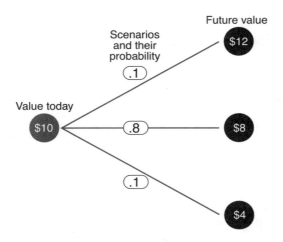

Figure 3.2. Mark-to-future for Fund B. *The initial stake, $10, is to be invested for one month. Thanks to possible events, such as movements in interest rates, there is a 10 per cent chance that the investment will rise to $12; an 80 per cent chance that it will fall to $8; and a 10 per cent chance that it will fall to $4.*

On the face of it, the set of outcomes posited in Fund B has more symmetry (10, 80, 10) than that attached to Fund A. The outcomes are more evenly weighted in Fund B. But on closer examination, the outcomes in Fund B are also heavily skewed on the downside. In fact, as most people can see intuitively, there is a 90 per cent chance that you will lose $2 or more of your initial investment. By comparison, Fund A offered only a 20 per cent chance that you might lose $2 or more.

Interestingly, some of the standard risk measures suggest that Fund B is less risky than Fund A (see figure 3.3). For instance, the volatility of Fund B is lower than that of Fund A. Fund B has a mean outcome of $8 and a volatility of 1.78, whereas Fund A, as we know, has a mean outcome of $10.80 and a volatility of 2.56. So, while Fund B has a lower volatility than Fund A, it has exactly the same VaR – both funds have a VaR of $6.

If you were to make your decision based upon two commonly used concepts of risk – variance and VaR – you might prefer Fund B over Fund A. This is despite the fact that Fund B also looks intuitively more

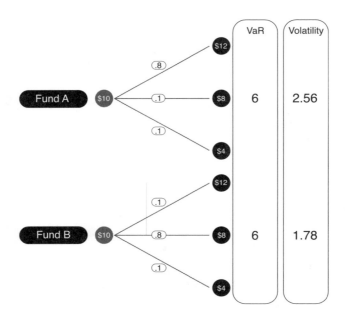

Figure 3.3. Mark-to-future for two funds. *This diagram summarizes the mark-to-future for two notional funds, showing how our initial investment of $10 will fare under different scenarios. The value-at-risk and volatility, two risk measures, are also shown.*

risky than Fund A – it has a far greater likelihood of delivering losses to its investors. So if you have $10, or $10,000, to allocate between these two funds, how would you decide between them and in what proportion? Standard investment theory would suggest that you put some money in each fund with more going to Fund B. But most people would probably follow their intuition and put all of their money in Fund A because they can see the obvious skew in their favour it represents. Positive skew is desirable; a negative skew is not. Volatility or value–at–risk might not capture skew and those using these measures will lose the benefit that can be gained by looking at a mark-to-future.

The fixed mathematics of volatility makes an assumption that is at odds with the real-world notion of skews: it assumes that the returns from Fund A are equally likely to be positive or negative, that they will be either up or down. Hence, according to the formula, the

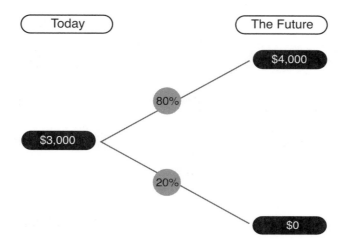

Figure 3.4. Investing a $3,000 gift. The initial value of your holdings is $3,000. If you invest it in the fund suggested by your broker, it may appreciate to $4,000 at some point in the future – or it may become worthless. The chance of it appreciating is 80 per cent; the chance of it losing all its value is 20 per cent.

higher the value assigned to volatility, the less attractive an investment looks. In the real world, however, most portfolios and funds are skewed. Their volatility may be relatively positive or negative. There simply is none of the neat symmetry of outcomes implied by the volatility approach to risk.

To set the stage for a more realistic approach, let's consider a simple problem involving financial risk. To make life interesting we will choose a problem that has confounded financial theorists for some time. It is adapted from the work of Daniel Kahneman and Amos Tversky, two influential academics who conducted pioneering work in the field of behavioural psychology and cognitive science.

Assume you receive a $3,000 gift. Your broker offers to invest it in a fund and she outlines the possibilities as follows. After one month the $3,000 will either increase to $4,000 with a likelihood of 80 per cent or will be worth zero with a 20 per cent likelihood. Should you accept the offer or keep your $3,000 and wait for another opportunity? How should you analyse the problem? Figure 3.4 shows the problem in the form of a scenario diagram.

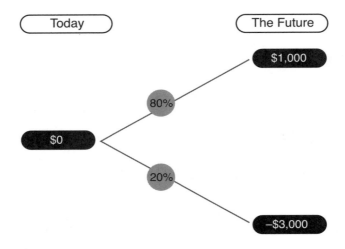

Figure 3.5. Adventures of a $3,000 investment. *This diagram shows the change in value of the $3,000 over time. The starting point — today — indicates $0, or no change. Change will occur only in the future. There is an 80 per cent probability of gaining $1,000, because the investment could increase to $4,000 under this scenario. There is also a 20 per cent chance that you could lose you entire investment of $3,000 if the second scenario occurs. The decision, therefore, as shown in the diagram, has an upside of $1,000 and a downside of $3,000.*

Another way of expressing the problem is in terms of the change in your position (see figure 3.5). If you choose to accept the offer and the result is that you lose everything, you will regret the decision. If, on the other hand, you end up with $4,000, you will have no regrets. Is the $1,000 gain worth the extra risk you will assume? Does it offset the potential regret of $3,000 you might experience? This problem was posed to a large group of people by Kahneman and Tversky, and they found that about 75 per cent of the respondents would not have invested in the fund and 25 per cent would have done so.

If you accept probability theory, you would invest instantly, because the average value of the bet is greater than $3,000. According to probability theory, the investment is worth 80 per cent of $4,000 plus 20 per cent of zero, which equals $3,200. This number, called the "expected value" or "mean," is higher than the $3,000 you would

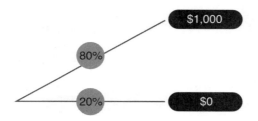

Figure 3.6. The upside. There is an 80 per cent chance of making $1,000.

have by not taking the investment. Another way of saying this would be that the odds are in your favour.

However, does this $3,200 figure really reflect the way most people would value this offer? Not according to the results obtained by Kahneman and Tversky.

The expected value indicates the average outcome if you were to make precisely the same choice hundreds of thousands of times. It does not indicate the value you should associate with the choice you face only once. As the experiments of Kahneman and Tversky have shown, real one-off decisions are not made by looking at probabilities alone. So how should you assess this decision? After all, despite its simplicity, it is much like all investment decisions we have to make.

Let's break the problem into two distinct parts: the upside and the downside. In valuing the upside, it may be helpful to think in terms of a bet; in valuing the downside, insurance may provide a model.

Imagine you were offered a bet that paid $1,000 with a probability of 80 per cent (see figure 3.6). How much is this bet worth to you? In other words, how much would you pay for the chance to partici- pate in winning the $1,000? Very few people would choose to pay $800, which is the expected or average value and is therefore what probability theory would deem to be fair. In fact, few people would pay an amount even close to this. Try it out on your friends. You will probably find it difficult to get anybody to pay much more than $100 to have an opportunity to take the bet. So this amount – say it is $100 – is the value of the upside to you. Different people will ascribe different values to such a bet, depending on their financial

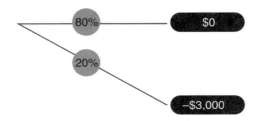

Figure 3.7. The downside. *There is a 20 per cent chance of losing $3,000.*

situation. A rich person is likely to pay more than a poor one for the same bet. If there were a market for such bets, with many participants, the market would ultimately come up with a fair price for the bet, which would be its objective value. In the absence of a market, the value is subjective.

In a similar way we can value the downside (see figure 3.7), this time using insurance as the paradigm. Imagine that you are faced with a potential loss of $3,000 with 20 per cent probability. How much, if anything, would you pay to insure against the loss? The richer you are, the more likely you are to self-insure – to pay nothing – since you can tolerate larger regret. As before, with the upside, very few people would be willing to pay $600 (the expected value equals $600, which is 20 per cent of $3,000) for this insurance. Let's for the sake of argument say you were willing to pay $120: this would then be your way of valuing the downside. If lots of people were simultaneously pricing this insurance, then there would be a market. If you wanted such insurance you would have to pay the market price.

By forcing you to place a value on the upside and downside of the investment, we are now able to give you a simple method for judging whether or not this investment is one you should make. The rule is simple. Subtract the cost of insuring the downside from the value of the upside and, if the net result is positive, make the investment. If it is negative, don't invest. In this example the upside was valued at $100 and we were prepared to pay $120 to insure the downside. The difference is − $20.

This value (upside value minus cost of insuring the downside) is what we will call the risk-adjusted value of the investment. An investment with positive risk-adjusted value is a good one. One with negative risk-adjusted value should be avoided. In the example given, the investment should be avoided because its risk-adjusted value is − $20.

You will notice that different people will come up with different answers based on their subjective assessment of the value of the upside bet and the downside insurance. If you believe that the insurance value of a potential loss of $3,000 with 20 per cent likelihood is only $80, then the risk-adjusted value of the investment would be $100 − $80 = $20. This is a positive number and the investment would look attractive to you. This explains why some people would invest in this fund while others would not.

Kahneman and Tversky also considered the mirror image of this example in their experiment in order to show that people react differently when they are already losing and could lose more. Once again their empirical results show that in two situations, which from a probabilistic or "rational" perspective are the same, people will react differently. People who are risk-averse in one situation turn into risk-seekers in a separate, seemingly equivalent, situation.

In their second example, you are having a bad time. You have already lost $3,000 when someone offers you an investment that could erase your loss with 80 per cent probability or lose you a further $1,000 with a 20 per cent probability. The expected value of the final position is − $3,200 (80 per cent of − $4,000 plus 20 per cent of zero). Probability theory would say this is less than the starting position so you should not invest. Yet empirical tests conducted by Kahneman and Tversky showed that most people would have invested. Why? (Notice that this "investment" is exactly the negative of the first case we considered.)

The scenario diagram for this situation is depicted in figure 3.8.

Let's assume the same person who valued the first investment applies consistent reasoning to this one. In the first case, the upside was $1,000 with 80 per cent probability and the downside was − $3,000 with 20 per cent probability. We suggested that the upside might be valued at $100 and the downside at − $120, giving a risk-adjusted value of − $20, so the decision was not to invest.

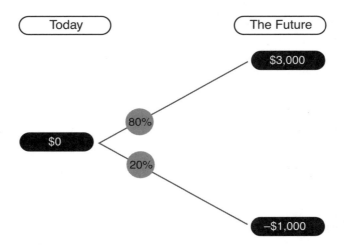

Figure 3.8. Further adventures of a $3,000 investment. This diagram shows the
change relative to the $3,000 you have lost. There is zero change ($0) today because
change will occur only in the future if you invest in the fund. There is an 80 per cent
probability of gaining $3,000 (since the loss would be erased). There is also a 20 per
cent chance that you will lose $1,000 more if the second scenario occurs. This decision
has an upside of $3,000 and a downside of − $1,000.

To be consistent, the same individual should apply the same discount factors for upside and downside in similar situations.
"Discount factors"? Before we can judge whether a value tomorrow is attractive to us, we have to know its value today. We also have
to calculate tomorrow's value using a discount factor that reflects
the time value of money − a dollar tomorrow is worth less than a
dollar today. If we think the difference will be 10 per cent, then we
apply that to tomorrow's value to gain a figure that is equivalent to
today's money.

In this case, our subject discounted the upside by 1/10 =
$100/$1,000 to get today's value and discounted the downside by
1/25 = $120/$3,000 to get today's value for the first investment problem. Applying the same logic to the second problem yields an upside
value of 1/10 x $3,000 = $300 and a downside value of 1/25 x − $1,000
= − $40. The risk-adjusted value of the second investment, consistent
with the analysis of the first investment, would be $300 − $40 = $260.

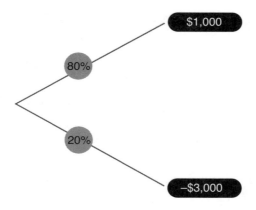

Figure 3.9. The buyer's view. There is an 80 per cent chance the deal will pay $1,000. The downside is that, with a probability of 20 per cent, the deal will lose $3,000.

A good investment. This is entirely consistent with the findings of Kahneman and Tversky and entirely inconsistent with the assumptions of formal economics!

The Kahneman and Tversky problem can also be analysed as the payoff facing the buyer and seller in a single deal. The buyer's and seller's perspective on the first example is shown in figures 3.9 and 3.10.

The buyer gains when the seller loses and vice versa. This is sometimes referred to as a zero-sum game. Why would two people enter into a deal like this, where the gain of one is the loss of the other? If the risk-adjusted value is negative for the buyer, is it not positive for the seller? This would be a lose–win situation, so you would expect one party always to shy away from the deal.

Wrong! There is a buyer and seller in each deal and each party believes the deal has a positive risk-adjusted value. That is, all deals are win–win, or else they would not be consummated. It is possible for deals to be win–win either because each party uses subjective assessments of the value of the upside and cost of insuring the downside or because the marginal effect of the deal on each individual's portfolio leads to different marginal upside and downside. So even when there is only one market price for every level of upside and downside it may still pay for two parties to trade!

In certain cases, such as investment decisions made in a mature

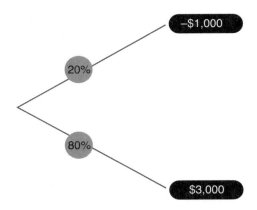

Figure 3.10. The seller's view. With a 20 per cent chance, this deal could lose
$1,000, but there is an 80 per cent chance it could make $3,000.

market, the upside and downside can be priced objectively by finding
portfolios with the exact same risk characteristics as the deal. In
financial economics this is known as a "complete market"; that is, one
in which we can always find the exact combination of financial
instruments to match any uncertain payoff we face. Suppose, for
example, a lottery was being offered to the public (see figure 3.11): for
an 80 per cent chance of winning $1,000 the tickets are priced at $300.
Then the upside would have a market (that is, objective) value of
$300. If, in addition, an insurance company is prepared to sell you a
policy costing $100 to cover you for a $3,000 loss, then the market
value of the downside is $100. The risk-adjusted value of the deal
would therefore be $300 − $100 = $200.

Notice that this scenario diagram looks much like the one in
figure 3.9. In fact, it has the same payoffs under the same conditions,
with the same probabilities. So in the market we have described,
where lotteries and insurance policies are available for the prices we
have used, the risk-adjusted value of the deal described above is the
true way in which it should be assessed. If we could sell the right
lottery ticket and buy the appropriate insurance policy, the payoff
possibilities would be exactly the same as in the deal we are evaluating. The lottery was worth $300 and the insurance policy could be

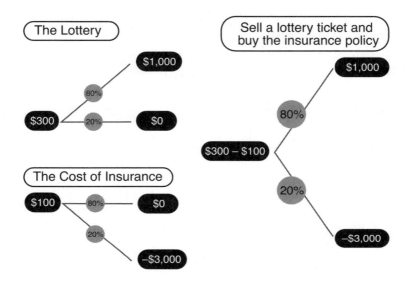

Figure 3.11. Combination lottery and insurance policy. *The payoffs are precisely the same as shown in figure 3.5.*

bought for $100, so the net (risk-adjusted) value of the deal is $200. This is a good deal because the risk-adjusted value is positive.

In practice, for most decisions we make, lotteries and insurance policies that exactly match the uncertain payoffs we face are not available. We do not usually operate in a complete market, so we need to make subjective estimates.

Almost any choice we face that has financial consequences has an upside and a downside. If it were all downside we would not enter into it voluntarily. If it were all upside everybody would want to do it and it wouldn't last long. The choice can be broken down into a bet (capturing the upside) and an insurance policy (capturing the downside). By accurately assessing the value of the bet and the insurance policy to you today, you can arrive at a risk-adjusted value, which is a proper assessment of the true value of the deal. A positive risk-adjusted value means that the deal is in your favour and you should probably participate. It does *not* mean that you are certain to profit from the transaction. A negative risk-adjusted value means that the deal is biased against you and should be avoided. It does not mean you will definitely lose money. Using risk-adjusted valuation is simply a sound, rational approach to financial transactions with an uncertain outcome. As we have seen, risk-adjusted valuation is quite different from looking at the average or expected value based on probabilities. It is not a guarantee that all your decisions will be on the winning side!

4

SWEET REGRET

Astute readers might have noticed that the word "regret" turned up in several of our earlier discussions. The power of regret comes from the fact that it makes formal what we feel or know intuitively about particular decisions. Because our analysis of risk, unlike standard views, embraces the concept of regret, it does not assume either that there is symmetry of outcomes or that we all feel the same whichever outcome occurs. To understand this, let us look again at Fund A, analysed in the previous chapter.

In this example (see figure 4.1), if interest rates rise, then as an investor you will have no regret because you have made money. If, on the other hand, rates stay the same, then you will lose $2 – something you will regret. And if rates fall, then you will have more regret than if rates had simply stayed the same. Your loss will be $6. Your benchmark for measuring how much regret you will feel is the $10 you

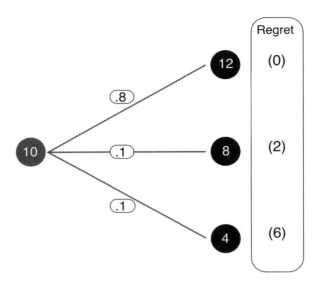

Figure 4.1. Mark-to-future for Fund A. One of these scenarios will occur in the future. If the first scenario occurs, you will have no regret because the fund will have increased in value. If the second scenario occurs, your regret will be 2 because your loss equals 2. Similarly, with the third scenario, regret equals 6.

began with (although, as we will see later, we could use another benchmark).

Now, because you do not know which of the three possible events will occur, it might help to calculate the average regret on Fund A. This is simple enough – multiply each outcome by its probability of occurring and then divide by the three outcomes. (We will see later that there might be better ways to "average out" over scenarios.) The answer is 0.8. But it is also a small number – in other words, you will not have much regret even assuming the worst outcome. It follows that you are not running a big downside risk.

By contrast, if regret is a large number, then you are probably running a big risk, insofar as that means the potential for large losses. Fund B, by this measure, has a greater regret than Fund A (see figure 4.2).

Put simply, regret can be a measure of your potential average loss.

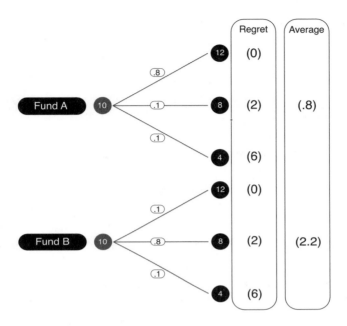

Figure 4.2. Mark-to-future for Funds A and B. The average regret is obtained by multiplying the probability of the scenarios by the regret value and summing up. Fund A has much less average regret than Fund B. In this sense, it is less risky, because it would cost less to insure.

Now, add what you know about regret to your earlier knowledge about volatility, and you clearly have a richer information set upon which to base an investment decision. In this case, calculations using these concepts would lead you to prefer Fund A over Fund B.

Another way to view regret that perhaps makes it even more convincing as a measure of risk is to compare it to insurance. Imagine that you can simultaneously purchase Fund A and purchase insurance on the downside. In the first scenario, the fund increases in value and there is no need for insurance. In the second scenario, the fund loses $2 (drops from $10 to $8) and the insurance company pays you $2. In the third scenario, the loss is $6 (drops from $10 to $4) and the insurance company pays you $6. In other words, the payoffs match your regret in each scenario. So we can view regret as equivalent to insuring the downside!

From this perspective, we can view regret as the amount of self-insurance we can tolerate. It represents a cutoff point below which we simply cannot bear the consequences of making a wrong decision, so we will go to great lengths to ascertain where the regret sets in. Beyond regret, our decision is more nuanced – our self-insurance vs. external-insurance dilemma is defined by our appetite for risk, as we shall see later in the book.

The concept of regret works in other contexts, too. Imagine that you have the opportunity to play in a lottery. For a bet of $1, you stand to win either $1 million or nothing. Should you play? If you choose not to play, you keep your $1. If you decide to play, then your average return will be almost zero – so perhaps on that basis alone you would not play. Similarly, because the volatility of this lottery is extremely high, you might also choose to avoid it. Just as with our two mutual funds, standard investment theory would tell you not to play this lottery.

However, with intuition as their guide, many, perhaps most, people would choose to play such a lottery. Why? Regret provides an explanation. Measured mathematically as well as practically, your regret in this instance is minimal.

You have a large upside if you win. Indeed, your potential upside is so high that you might even forego eating a sandwich in order to play the lottery. If you lose, chances are that your loss won't break the bank. Even though the chances of winning are very small, the lottery has an outcome that is skewed in your favour, because your downside is so small.

Imagine another lottery with exactly the same odds, but in which the prize is $10 billion and a single ticket costs $10,000. For many people this would be a far more difficult proposition. For someone of modest means, it might be impossible to raise the stake. And for those who could raise the money at a stretch, the regret of losing would be considerable. Many people might therefore choose not to play.

However, those who could afford the stake might prefer the second lottery over the first because its upside is so much bigger. For them, the appeal of the bigger upside would outweigh the regret even though the potential regret is much greater. This leads to another feature of regret. How much regret people feel varies depending upon their circumstances. Regret is a measure which recognizes that the context in which choices are made is an important factor in determining why different people choose to act differently – it is sensitive to our unique circumstances.

Regret is not the same as disappointment. David Bell, a professor at Harvard, makes a neat distinction between the two. Imagine your boss has just called you in and told you that your reward for an excellent year's performance is a $5,000 bonus. Are you pleased? Yes, probably elated, especially if you were not expecting anything. But if you were expecting a $10,000 bonus, then you will be disappointed. In other words, your prior expectations, or benchmark, dictate how you feel. The higher your expectations, the greater the disappointment. Regret, says Professor Bell, is a psychological reaction to making a wrong decision, where wrong is determined by actual outcomes rather than on the information available at the time the decision was made. Put simply, if our benchmark for disappointment is our prior expectations, our benchmark for regret is the outcome that would have resulted from a different choice. The stress is on the consequences of decisions rather than on the probabilities of particular outcomes.

Is this distinction between regret and disappointment really meaningful? Certainly. Imagine a lottery that gives you a fifty-fifty chance of winning $0 or $10. If you play and lose, then you will feel disappointment. But if you chose the same lottery over an alternative lottery that offered a sure $4, then you would feel both disappointment and regret. (Interestingly, it is possible to suffer regret without disappointment. This happens if the outcome of our choices exactly matches our expectations, but is less than we could have obtained from an alternative choice.)

Professor Bell also makes a neat distinction between risk and regret. Imagine that you regularly play a lottery and always pick the same combination of numbers. One week, out of boredom, you alter your numbers. You are still exposed to the same risk – your action has not changed the odds by one iota – but you have exposed yourself to enormous regret. Think how you would feel if your old numbers were to win in the very week you switched!

Decisions, Decisions

The idea of regret has long been familiar to two types of economists whose interests overlap. The first is a group known as decision theorists. Decision theory has a long history. It is a field with close ties to risk management – clearly, how we decide things is informed in part by our expectations of and appetites for the outcomes we expect from our chosen course of action. In economics, however, not all decision theory has been sensitive to risk-management concerns. Indeed, many economists have been fixated on an abstraction, the so-called economic "agent" who is determined to maximize "utility" and makes decisions accordingly. (One of the failures of formal economics has been its use of jargon, but we hope the last sentence will be clear to most readers).

In decision theory, the idea of regret is used as a tool for formalizing the thought processes required when we face difficult decisions. Technically these are known as "decisions under uncertainty." Now, this goes to the very heart of our subject. We cannot predict the future. So how do we decide? Well, we might consider the likely consequences for us in the event of particular outcomes (scenarios). Indeed, we might give greater weight to those potential consequences than we do to any probability-based assessment of likely outcomes.

George Shackle thought that we would be influenced by what he termed "potential surprise": the nastier the surprise, the stronger our aversion to it. He attacked the idea that we should assign probabilities to possible outcomes as a basis for decisions by making a telling observation. Assume that you think there will be three possible outcomes in future and that you assign an equal one-third probability to each one. Then a surprise event occurs that raises the possibility of a fourth outcome. Does it suddenly make sense to alter the probabilities you have previously assigned to the other outcomes? If the answer is yes, then surely those original probabilities were wrong.

So, how can we use regret to help us make decisions? When governments make policy decisions, they have to weigh today's real costs against tomorrow's uncertain benefits. By attaching probabilities to future events (an act that changes uncertainty into risk), we can usually calculate what is known as our "net present benefit" and use that as the basis for our decision. But we know that there are many occasions when it is impossible to attach useful probabilities to an unknowable future, so we have to find ways to model the uncertainty we face.

Harry M. Markowitz, a Nobel laureate in economics, dealt neatly with the issue when he answered a question about retirement planning put to him by *Money* magazine. "I should have computed the historical co-variances of the asset classes and drawn an efficient frontier," he said. "Instead, I visualized my grief if the stock market went way up and I wasn't in it – or if it went way down and I was completely in it. My intention was to minimize my future regret. So I split my contributions fifty-fifty between bonds and equities."

A more serious example concerns the British government's preoccupation during 1995-96 with so-called mad cow disease and the danger that it had mutated into forms that can infect humans. Even as we were writing this book in late 1997, the government banned the sale of beef on the bone, fearing the possible infection of consumers by a dementia-like condition. To many this seemed an extreme step, for the risk of infection appeared to be relatively small. (Ironically, around the same time the health authorities in Hong Kong ordered the slaughter of 1 million chickens because they feared that a small outbreak of a new form of influenza could become an epidemic.) How much should be done today to limit the risk that there could be another, bigger outbreak of the disease in humans? A big outbreak undoubtedly would represent a major public health disaster and could cost many billions to manage. Equally, however, taking all the steps now to eradicate the disease would certainly put a huge strain on public finances. This is particularly intriguing because

Cost Matrix	Zero	Low	Medium	High
Do nothing	0	20	50	100
Mild intervention	10	20	35	60
Strong intervention	40	42	45	50

Figure 4.3. Assumptions about infectivity (scenarios). *For example, if the infectivity is low and the government invokes a strong intervention, then the future cost would be 42.*
Source: The Economist

politicians who decide policy suffer from a unique form of regret –
they can be blamed by voters either for acting or for not acting and
booted out of office! Hence the occasional tendency to act, even if
the risk appears relatively insignificant.

Here is how decision theorists approach such a problem using
regret (see figure 4.3). They begin by constructing a cost matrix. This
one uses simple arbitrary units to illustrate the point, but it can be
done with real numbers, particularly in a case that involves known
scientific probabilities. The cost matrix lines up assumptions about
how likely it is that humans will be infected against three policy
options: do nothing; undertake mild intervention in the form of
selective culling of cattle; and undertake strong intervention in the
form of a complete cull. If the disease does not infect humans and the
government does nothing, then its net cost is zero. Assume that the
cost of mild intervention is 10, while strong intervention costs 40 –
that completes the first column of the matrix. To fill in the rows, start
at the top by assuming that a low rate of infection will cost 20, a
medium rate 50, and a high rate 100. The lower rows are completed
by assuming that selective culling reduces the likelihood of infection
by 50 per cent, while a total cull will reduce it by 90 per cent.

Now the matrix can be used to guide our thinking. And we can
use it to convey our appetite for risk. If we are feeling lucky, we might
choose the "minimim" – the minimum of minimums. In this case,
we would choose the "do nothing" option that will cost us nothing,

Regret Matrix	Zero	Low	Medium	High
Do nothing	0	0	15	50
Mild intervention	10	0	0	10
Strong intervention	40	22	10	0

Figure 4.4. Assumptions about infectivity (with regret). For example, if the infectivity is low and the government invokes a strong intervention, then the regret would be 22.
Source: The Economist

provided it turns out that infectivity is zero. But it will cost us more than any other policy (i.e. 100) if the rate of infectivity is high. If we are hyper-cautious, then we might choose the "minimax" – the minimum of maximums. For each policy, we ask what the worst result could be and then choose the policy that offers the best of these bad outcomes. The worst result for do nothing is 100, for mild intervention is 60, and for strong intervention is 50. We would choose strong intervention. This is the "best of a bad lot" philosophy.

This is where regret comes in. Underneath our cost matrix we can compile a regret matrix (see figure 4.4). This is calculated by asking which policy produces the best result for each of the infectivity assumptions in turn. Then we compare the results of the other two policies with that best result and we regard the difference in cost as a measure of our regret. For example, the best result for medium infectivity is a cost of 35 from mild intervention. In our regret matrix, then, that would be zero. The cost of doing nothing is 50, so if we choose that policy we will be 50 − 35 worse off than if we choose the best policy – hence the 15 scored in the matrix. The cost of strong intervention is 45, so that scores 10 in our regret matrix.

Now we can apply our minimax decision rules as before. For each policy, which outcome would we regret most? For do nothing, it is a cost of 50 if infectivity turns out to be high. For mild intervention, it is a cost of 10 if infectivity turns out to be zero or high. And for strong intervention, it is a cost of 40 if infectivity turns out to be zero.

Minimax regret chooses the policy that gives the lowest of these results. In other words, it is not putting a floor under disaster itself, but under how bad we are going to feel if things go wrong. Clearly in this case we would choose mild intervention. This approach to decision-making has not created certainty where none existed. But, thanks to regret, it has created a structured way of thinking about an otherwise intractable problem.

Notice that implicitly we have used a special benchmark, namely the "best possible" event under a given scenario. This is where we have used poetic licence when using the word regret. For decision theorists this is *the* benchmark. We allow *any* benchmark when defining regret.

Behaving Ourselves

The second group of economists who are familiar with the idea of regret comprises behavioural economists. In essence, behavioural economists try to adapt standard economics and finance to take into account how people behave in the real world. Behavioural economics is a controversial field, partly because it stretches the normally abstract domain of economics into areas that are of widespread interest, like psychology and cognitive science. But it is also a rewarding field because its proponents are trying to do something intuitively smart: they are trying to build models of economic behaviour that capture more of the real world with all its kinks and rough edges. We have already examined one famous experiment by two pioneers of behavioural economics – Amos Tversky and Daniel Kahneman.

To a behavioural economist, regret is a concept that captures the frustration or despair we feel when bad things happen. Meir Statman, a leading professor in the field, relates the following example. Imagine there are two identical roads that lead to your home. Habitually you take the high road. But one day for no particular reason you take the low road and you crash your car. Compare how you feel with how you would have felt if instead you had crashed on the normal road home. The risk you ran and the outcome were essentially similar. The higher sense of frustration you feel because you changed your normal pattern is regret.

Behavioural economists are intrigued by how feelings such as regret affect people's behaviour. In investing, for instance, many people have closed bank accounts in favour of investment accounts that function like ordinary chequing accounts but allow liquid funds to be invested in the stock market. Often holders of these accounts will defer writing a cheque because they want to keep their money exposed to the possibility of rising prices – they would feel regret if they missed out on an upswing in the market.

One of the most interesting aspects of behavioural economics is its effort to understand so-called "cognitive biases," quirks in the way people think that can lead them to do things that on the surface appear illogical, inconsistent, or just plain wrong-headed. One telling example is the difficulty we have in framing questions correctly so that we are divining useful answers. The average investor, for instance, probably knows nothing or very little about the central theories of modern finance. Those theories tell informed investors that they are unlikely to outperform the stock market on a consistent basis over time. But the vast majority of investors think or at least hope that they will beat the market. Why? If they were behaving logically, then many of these investors would be better off taking their money and investing it elsewhere, perhaps in tax-exempt bonds or an index fund.

The answer, according to behavioural economists such as Professor Statman, is that we are all affected by biases: "In most investors' case, they simply cannot see that they are the suckers in the game. The real suckers are the ones who think they can divine inside information from the *Wall Street Journal*. For example they might read an article about aging baby boomers who need bifocals and think they can make a buck by buying shares in an eyewear company," he remarks. "But they are usually just observing something that lots of other people already know."

Investors are often deceived by their tendency to frame basic questions wrongly. Consider the story about two hikers who are walking along a path when they encounter a tiger. One turns to the other and says, "There's no point in running, that tiger is much faster than both of us." "I disagree," replies the other. "The question is not how fast we are relative to the tiger, but whether I'm faster than you."

Then consider an investor who wants to buy options on the Japanese yen. Professor Statman says the investor should ask: "What do I know about the yen, the trade deficit, and so on, that dozens of professional economists and currency traders don't know?" The answer would persuade most people not to make the investment. But people ask the wrong questions and go on investing. As Professor Statman jokes, this phenomenon is probably the salvation of the market. Or, as Mark Twain once wrote: "Let us be thankful for the fools. But for them the rest of us could not succeed."

If these sound like abstractions, then consider the case of Microsoft Man, whose story appeared in *Grant's Interest Rate Observer*, a newsletter on financial markets. Microsoft Man worked in the computer industry. Before he became Microsoft Man he owned a group of well-regarded and somewhat conservative mutual funds that had been assembled for him by a respected firm of money managers. Then one day he bought a few shares in Microsoft. The shares performed better than his funds, so one by one, over a period of ten months, Microsoft Man sold all his funds and bought more and more shares in Microsoft. Finally, he owned only Microsoft shares, at which point the fund managers suggested that they no longer wanted his business. The newsletter remarked in mid-1997, "To date, of course, he has had no cause for regret."

Why might Microsoft Man suffer from regret? Believing he knows better than his professional advisers do, he has broken a cardinal rule of finance theory by putting all of his eggs in a single basket. Assume Microsoft shares tumble at some point: our investor will suddenly find that his lack of diversification is extremely costly. At that point, he might remember the more balanced holdings he once owned. His regret will be enormous.

Often, regret creeps into everyday language. Alan Greenspan, chairman of America's Federal Reserve Bank, has an unenviable job. With his colleagues on the Federal Open Market Committee, he must set interest rates so that America's economy neither rushes into an inflationary boom nor collapses into a recession. This involves guessing (sorry, forecasting) where the economy is heading. When he testified to Congress in mid-1997, he used an analogy to describe the difficulty of operating in an uncertain world: "A driver might tap the brakes to make sure not to be hit by a truck coming down the street, even if he thinks the chances of such an event are relatively low; the costs of being wrong are simply too high. Similarly, in conducting monetary policy the Federal Reserve needs constantly to look down the road to gauge the future risks to the economy and act accordingly." Thus has regret been officially endorsed by the world's top central banker!

We can gain more insight into regret from other examples drawn from behavioural economics. Suppose you have bought two $100 tickets to a show at a theatre that is a two-hour drive from your home. Just before you are due to set off a nasty snowstorm begins. Driving will be hazardous. Do you make the trip? Most people would say yes – you have already spent $200, so you will make the effort. The $200 you have spent is "sunk cost" that you are loath to sacrifice. But what if you had intended to buy tickets at the box office just before the performance? Then you would feel far happier about not travelling. You would probably even turn down an offer of $200 payable if you were to make the trip. You feel far more comfortable about "losing" that $200 than you do about "losing" the same amount of money by not using tickets you had already bought. Or, in reverse, you would have far greater regret if the storm caused you to miss the show when you had already bought tickets than if you passed on the chance to be paid $200 to attend the theatre.

Regret also sheds light on the question of why people often behave like each other – they "follow the crowd." This phenomenon has been particularly evident in stock markets, where the tendency of investors to behave like a pack has often caused wild gyrations. Nowhere is this more true than in the United States. A generation of future retirees has poured money into stocks, pushing indices such as the Dow Jones Industrial Average and the Standard & Poor's 500 to ever new highs. Writers and commentators have tended to describe this behaviour as irrational. Investors are said to be infected by a mania that drives them into a frenzy of activity; then, when reality dawns, the mania ends in a rush for the exit.

But what if regret is at work? It is easy to see that many of us find some comfort from being in the same boat as others. Indeed, it is hard to find a genuine contrarian – someone truly prepared to go it alone and to live with the consequences (which can include ridicule). Perhaps we feel less regret when we all fall together. If the stock market crashes, and our portfolio with it, our regret may be lessened by the knowledge that millions of others suffered with us.

Even professional investors' behaviour can be analysed using regret. It is well known, for instance, that fund managers like to do only a little better than their competitors, but hate to do either really well or really badly. Clients are suspicious of managers whose returns stray too far from the average. And when a fund manager takes a contrarian stance, the regret can be enormous. In Britain, for example, one leading fund manager lost large amounts of assets under management after publicly expressing the view that shares were wildly overvalued and switching towards bonds. That stance was not only wrong, but also exposed the firm in question to large regret in the form of lost business. Other fund managers who watched this debacle probably felt it strengthen their intuition that it is best to be safely tucked in among the herd!

The same might be true of investment analysts, those highly paid experts whose job it is to assess the value of publicly traded companies. Only rarely does an analyst stick out her neck and issue a "sell" recommendation on a stock rated a "buy" by most of her peers. In addition to the flak that this can cause from the company concerned, the reason is simple. Her regret for being wrong will be immense. It is much safer to be late and right than early and wrong!

No wonder many traditional economists have a problem with behavioural economic analysis – it's fun!

Although they differ in how much weight they accord to human foibles, both decision theorists and behaviourists try to understand how we make decisions – what motivates us, what scares us, what exhilarates us. And both are trying to face up to the tension between risk and uncertainty. If we rely too heavily on probabilities and "utility maximization" to guide our decisions, then we will likely end up suffering regret. But in order to manage the risks that lie ahead of us, we must make attempts to reduce uncertainty. Regret recognizes that we care about the consequences of our decisions, and that offered a bet with known probabilities, some of us might choose not to play because we could not stand the consequences of losing. Although regret has been discussed in economic and financial theory, it has never been placed at centre stage in the way that we are seeking to promote it. We hope to show that it deserves a place among the key concepts of risk management and risk analysis.

Regret can show us how our concern about downside risk (that is, losing money or losing more than we can afford) might guide us towards one choice over another, directing us towards investments that we intuitively feel more comfortable with than those that might be recommended by other commonly used risk-management techniques such as mean variance and value-at-risk (VaR).

However, a really useful measure of risk is one that also takes into account potential upside returns (that is, making money!). We can construct now a range of scenarios showing the varying degrees we would experience in each case. But how should we account for the expectation that we might also make money under our scenarios? How do we reach a truly balanced view of our expectations about the future?

First, for the sake of argument, let's see how regret itself, though an improvement on other techniques for measuring risk, can be imperfect. Here are two portfolios that have the same regret, but different potential (upside) returns (see figure 4.5). Incidentally they have the same value-at-risk as well.

How do we account for the fact that one portfolio has significantly better upside than the other, even though they both have the same regret? The answer lies in the fact that, acting like typical investors, we have separated the processes of how we measure risk and how we select our investments. When we measure only risk, we usually think in terms of the downside – how we can avoid losses. But when we invest in a stock or mutual fund, we focus primarily on our potential returns. We ask ourselves, "What is the upside and how does it

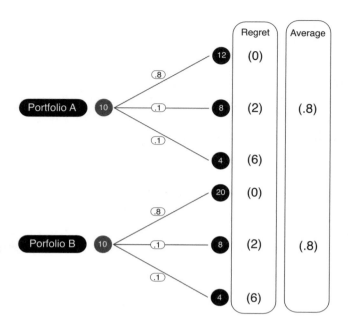

Figure 4.5. Regret remains constant. *These two portfolios have significantly different potential returns, but the regret in each case is exactly the same.*

compare to what else is available?" However, it is also clear that we balance this implicitly or explicitly with the potential for regret. If we did not, we would be like Microsoft Man and simply put all our eggs in the best-looking basket.

Think what the separation of measurement and selection means – we give too much weight to regret in the first instance, and too much weight to upside in the second. This means that at the heart of our investment process are two mistakes – no wonder we are often surprised by the results of our decisions! Similarly, think of a business and how it allocates capital between its different operations and it should be obvious that a coherent system of risk management must include a unified approach to measurement and selection.

We have already argued that regret is an improvement on traditional measures of risk. Can we go further? We can, by developing a way to reconnect our measurement of risk with our selection of portfolios or allocation of capital. The necessary next step is to refine the

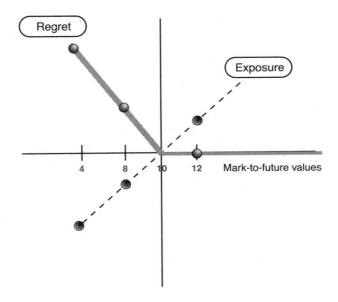

Figure 4.6. Risk-adjusted return. *The black points on the tree diagram represent three potential outcomes for our initial stake of $10. In this example, our $10 is both the portfolio's current value and the benchmark against which we measure the different outcomes. This diagram is an alternate way of viewing figure 3.2.*

notion of risk-adjusted return that we outlined previously. First, we need to make our description of regret a little more formal. We can illustrate regret by showing what it looks like for the simple choice we introduced in Chapter 3 (see figure 4.6). At the centre is the $10 we have in hand. The three points show the potential outcomes. "Regret" is the bold line that offsets the negative outcomes.

To calculate regret we take the following steps.

1. Subtract the benchmark from the portfolio value for each scenario outcome.
2. If it is negative (i.e., a loss with respect to the benchmark) then:
   (a) take the negative of this number (the negative of a negative is positive) and it is the regret;

(b) if, however, the difference between the portfolio and benchmark happens to be positive (i.e., again, over the benchmark), then set the regret to zero.

Measured over all scenarios that would cause losses, average regret is the average of the difference between our chosen portfolio and our chosen benchmark. If the portfolio exceeds the benchmark, then we have no regret. But when our portfolio underperforms the benchmark, then we can measure our regret. Finance professionals looking at our picture of this downside exposure will see that the regret function looks like a "put" option that has a maturity equal to the time horizon of our investment. In fact, if we could only price it correctly, that put option would perfectly describe our regret because it would cost the same as it should cost in theory to insure against the same level of downside risk.

(If you own a "put" option, it means that you can pass on a loss-making exposure to whoever sold you the option, so long as your loss occurs within a specified period of time. For our purposes, the important point is that a put option neatly captures how we feel about insuring the downside. Similarly, a "call" option allows us to capture the upside.)

Notice that we have slipped in the idea of insurance again. In some circumstances, such as this one, risk and insurance are nearly equivalent. If we could take out an insurance policy against our downside risk, then the premium or price of that insurance ought to be the same as the price of a put option on that amount of loss. In effect, insurance can eliminate risk (with the qualification that we remain exposed to the insurer's ability to pay any claims). Thus the cost of insurance should be equivalent to the value we need to place on the risk it eliminates.

Before we can go further, we need to introduce some ideas drawn from modern finance theory. One important idea has its origins in pioneering work conducted in the 1950s by Merton Miller and Franco Modigliani on firms' capital structures – that is, the proportion of debt and equity firms hold – and whether they affect stock market values. Modigliani and Miller showed how in a world without taxes there is no optimal proportion of debt and equity that maximizes a firm's market value. If there were, then any divergence from the optimal level would swiftly be priced away by traders.

Merton Miller himself gives an amusing description of the "M&M theorem." "You understand the M&M theorem if you understand why this is a joke: the pizza delivery man comes to Yogi Berra after the game and says, 'Yogi, how do you want this pizza cut, into quarters or eighths?' Yogi says, 'Cut it into eight pieces, I'm feeling hungry tonight.'" The joke is in the fact that the number and shape of the pieces doesn't affect the size of the pizza. Similarly, the stocks, bonds, warrants etc. that have been issued don't affect the aggregate value of the firm. They just slice up the underlying earnings in different ways.

Modigliani and Miller went on to generate a host of related finance theories. Another of their propositions is central to our argument. To show that the stock market would price away any difference from some notionally optimal capital structure, the economists used the notion of "arbitrage." The simplest way to understand arbitrage is to go back a few years before computers and telephones sped up financial transactions. Savvy and well-equipped traders could monitor the price of gold in London and the price in Hong Kong, buying and selling in each place to exploit any small differences. In conducting this "temporal arbitrage," the traders would cause prices to fall back into line.

Other forms of arbitrage have now supplanted the temporal kind, largely because technology in the developed world has drastically reduced the time within which prices in two different physical locations can stray from parity. However, many finance theorists and economists have embraced an apparently peculiar idea: that we live in a world of no arbitrage. As Steve Ross, a leading financial economist at Yale, puts it, "That means there are no possibilities for true arbitrage in this stock market, in any of the markets, even underdeveloped markets. It is not possible to borrow at 10 per cent and lend at 12 per cent." How can this be? And isn't it equivalent to the joke about the economist who saw a $50 bill on the ground but refused to pick it up on the assumption that it could not possibly be there because someone else would already have picked it up?

In fact, the idea of no arbitrage is not as crazy as it sounds. And it is very useful for our risk framework. In essence, it says that for most participants in a market there can be no arbitrage because any openings will have disappeared before they can react. Think about it. If you are an investor, even a large one, what chance do you have of spotting and exploiting an arbitrage? Even assuming you spot one, it is likely that by the time you can act, market professionals will have forced prices back into line. And if there is a persistent anomaly, you run the risk that what you are entering is not an opportunity for arbitrage but a price relationship that has incorporated new information and is therefore different.

For another way of thinking about no arbitrage, imagine that you have two investment opportunities, each with a different interest rate. Once you adjust each opportunity for risk, then in a world of no arbitrage the two opportunities are paying the same rate of interest. If you choose an investment that carries a higher interest rate, then you are taking risk relative to something with a lower interest rate.

Recall now that regret is equivalent to a put option on our downside exposure. In order to ensure that the option can be properly priced, we have to assume a world of no arbitrage.

We have already noted that regret as a downside measure is only half the picture. We also need to consider our potential upside. Indeed, just as there is an expression for regret, so there is one for upside.

Instead of looking at the average over loss-making scenarios, we look at the average over those scenarios with upside – those in which our portfolio outperforms the benchmark. Not surprisingly, given our earlier picture of downside regret, upside looks just like a "call" option on our net exposure with a maturity equal to our time horizon (see figure 4.7). All the future benefits we expect from owning this set of investments are captured by this option. In some sense, it represents the best you could do from owning this portfolio. For that reason it has interesting pricing characteristics. You won't value it higher than the upside it represents to you because that is the most it is worth. So we know the price of the call option that is upside and we know why we will not pay more than it is worth.

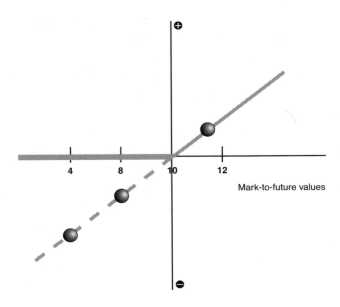

Figure 4.7. The Upside. *The upside is zero when the portfolio underperforms the benchmark; otherwise it is positive. This figure of the upside captures all the points at which our chosen portfolio outperforms our benchmark.*

Upside is a powerfully seductive concept. Investors who look only at upside and pay no regard to regret have a dangerously tilted view of the world. Yet, thanks to the way fund managers are allowed to advertise their performance, this is exactly what millions of people are encouraged to do. A glance at the advertisements for mutual funds in the financial press soon reveals that they are dominated by the upside. Regret scarcely gets a look in.

What if we adopt an all-round view of our exposure by considering both regret and upside? Then we will have a picture of our net performance. It works as follows:

U = Upside, which is equivalent to a call option on our future outperformance;

R = Downside (regret), which is equivalent to insurance or a put option.

So long as $U - R$ is a positive number, then we should want to hold the portfolio. We call this the "market value" of the deal. (When investment bankers talk of "marking a portfolio to market," they mean adjusting its value to reflect changes in market prices.) Put another way, if U is greater than R, then we should like the deal we are being offered because the upside value is worth more than the cost of insuring the downside. We should make more than we will lose.

Intuitively we are always assessing such net exposures in our heads. Imagine you are offered a partnership in a law firm. Although you might not quantify the decision, you will almost certainly remember that your rewards (U) might be offset by the liabilities you will take on as a partner (R). These days, many directors of firms have to weigh their share options (U) against the danger that they might be subjected to a shareholder lawsuit (R). Firms can make directorships more attractive by adjusting regret using directors' insurance.

Measuring our Hunger for Risk

We have argued that the concepts of regret and upside greatly improve our ability to think coherently about risk. We have also asserted that regret is more useful than existing risk measures because it can reflect our appetite for risk. We need to explore in more detail how this works in practice. And to do that we need to introduce the concept of risk-adjusted value – value that has been altered to take into account our personal attitude towards risk. In some circumstances we are more prone to risk than others. To reflect these differences in our behaviour, we introduce a "risk-aversion constant"; let's call it lambda (λ), a symbol for the eleventh letter of the Greek alphabet.

Another way to think of lambda is as a margin or insurance premium that we might set aside against our possible losses in the event that our upside fails to materialize. The larger the value for lambda, the more risk-averse the decision-maker since she is paying a higher price to self-insure the risk. People who only take the risk into account when making a deal essentially have very high lambdas. Typically lambda is greater than 1, since otherwise we are in effect paying less than the cost of insurance to cover the risk and will not be

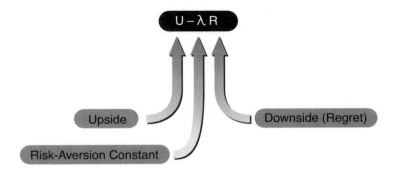

Figure 4.8. Risk-adjusted value. The upside minus lambda (or risk-aversion constant) multiplied by the downside or regret yields the risk-adjusted value. Lambda, typically, is greater than 1 because we usually are risk-averse.

adequately covered. Another way of saying this is that most people would like to have the assurance that they've set aside sufficient funds to protect their downside. Most of us are risk-averse! On the other hand, when a decision is largely based on the upside, the decision-maker discounts risk with a very small lambda. If our lambda is less than 1, then we will be paying our counterparty for the privilege of taking on risk, something that happens when we feel especially bullish. Such people are referred to as risk-seekers.

Investment counsellors often recommend that we split our funds in a pyramid fashion, with a small portion going to risky investments (low lambda), a larger portion going to mutual funds (medium lambda), and the bulk in safe investments such as bonds (high lambda). In effect we set the lambda for each portion of our holdings and purchase the best investments for each. We maximize the risk-adjusted value $(U - \lambda R)$ for that portion of the fund.

A valuable refinement of lambda is the "implied lambda." Once we know that a deal has been done, it is easy to work out the implied risk appetite of the counterparties. Assume we observe a deal, with an upside equal to U and regret equal to R. It must mean that the decision-maker has placed a positive value on $(U - \lambda R)$. Therefore the allowance she has made for risk aversion (lambda) is less than the upside divided by regret.

A natural framework, analogous to the no-arbitrage framework of finance mentioned earlier, assumes that every risky deal that is executed and every decision involving risk that is acted upon is win–win for both sides. In other words, both parties must be viewing the deal from the perspective that it has positive risk-adjusted value or else they would not enter into it. Thus each party has an implied lambda that satisfies:

$$U - \lambda R \text{ greater than zero}$$

Implied lambdas are another way of expressing the same fact. We can solve the above equation to find the party's implied lambda, that is, the risk-aversion constant that he had to have assumed in order to go ahead with the deal. In complete markets U and R are unique and thus the same for both parties. In incomplete markets, as we saw earlier, each party might have their own value for U and R.

In a complete market, one party's regret is the other party's upside and vice versa.[*] This means that one party must be a risk-taker and the other risk-averse with respect to this single deal. However, people hardly ever make deals in isolation. So the individual deal will be measured as to how it affects the upside and regret of the deal-maker's *overall* holdings. If the deal improves the risk-adjusted value of these overall holdings then it is a good one.

This portfolio effect is one of the most important features of financial and business risk. It explains why some people can afford deals that others cannot. It also explains why many transactions that might seem uneconomic can occur in the real world. Where one party holds a portfolio which contains an offsetting position or asset, it is possible to conduct business that benefits both parties. Often we overlook the portfolio dimension of our decisions. This can result in the systematic mispricing of deals and, consequently, poor risk management.

---

[*] If there are two parties, A and B, for a deal to be win–win, the implied lambda must satisfy: λA less than U/R and λB less than R/U.

To understand the power of lambda, think of how we select a mutual fund today. Assume that we wish to choose from the very best funds appropriate to our investment needs. As we will see in Chapter 7, there is lots of information we need before we can make an informed choice, but remarkably little useful information available. However, let's assume for the moment that we want a single number that will indicate how we might choose among a small number of options.

What data are available to inform our choice? Typically we are offered two bits of information. The first tells us a fund's absolute performance over the last year – a simple twelve-month percentage total return. The second gives us a measure of the fund's return against its chosen benchmark (known as "beta," this tells how much the fund has fluctuated compared to its benchmark). This information tells us how volatile the fund has been relative to its peers.

Both of these numbers are historical. They show how the fund has performed in the recent past. We now know, however, that a useful measure of risk looks forward rather than backwards, that historical trends cannot with confidence be projected into the future.

Using modern risk management and regret, a particular investment option can look different depending upon your appetite for risk, provided the latter takes into account both your downside aversion and your upside hopes. To illustrate this, let us look at how we might choose among competing mutual funds. Let us imagine three rival funds:

Fund A has an expected upside of \$10 and a possible downside of \$5.
Fund B has an expected upside of \$30 and a possible downside of \$40.
Fund C has an expected upside of \$15 and a possible downside of \$5.

The power of our U − R (risk-adjusted) analysis is that it recognizes our intuition: we feel differently about particular choices depending

upon the relative weight we place on the upside and the downside –
in other words, how risky we think the world is. The greater our tolerance for risk, the less attention we will pay to the downside. If we
are assessing a mutual fund as a potential element in our stable of
speculative investments, we will be relatively unconcerned about
events that might cause large temporary losses. But if the fund is to
be part of our core, long-term holdings, we will place correspondingly greater stress on downside risk – we will give lambda a high
value because we will be biased against funds with big downside risk.

(Incidentally, the above paragraph contains a classic example of
what behavioural economists call "framing." Can you spot it? The
answer is at the end of the chapter.)

Let us assign three values to lambda that reflect varying attitudes
towards risk. The higher the value, the more we feel disinclined to
take on risk:

1. We actively seek risk: lambda = 0.2
2. We are neutral: lambda = 1
3. We are very risk-averse: lambda = 5

Now, apply each value for lambda to each of our choice of funds.

Risk-adjusted Valuation for Three Funds

    Fund A: 1. 10 − (5 x 0.2) = 9
            2. 10 − (5 x 1) = 5
            3. 10 − (5 x 5) = −25

    Fund B: 1. 30 − (40 x 0.2) = 22
            2. 30 − (40 x 1) = −10
            3. 30 − (40 x 5) = −170

    Fund C: 1. 15 − (5 x 0.2) = 14
            2. 15 − (5 x 1) = 10
            3. 15 − (5 x 5) = −10

Clearly, if we are risk-averse, i.e. case 3 (our lambda is 5), we will tend to avoid Fund B. Even though it has the greatest potential upside, it has a significant probability of large regret (170). In fact, we will greatly prefer Fund C since it has the highest risk-adjusted value (− 10). Fund A also gives off a powerful signal that its downside risk is significant in relation to its potential upside.

If our attitude towards risk is neutral, i.e. case 2, then we might choose Fund C, which has the highest risk-adjusted return (equal to 10). Its upside is closely mirrored by its downside: our expectation of a positive return is offset by the possibility of an equal loss. But the extent of the potential loss is limited, hence our relative lack of concern.

If we are actively seeking risk and give greater weight to our potential return than to our possible losses, i.e. case 1, lambda will lead us to Fund B.

If we can use lambda to help us choose between three funds depending on our tolerance for risk, then there seems little practical barrier against its use as a general means of making relative rather than absolute choices pertaining to risk. We can use lambda, for example, to judge whether we have sufficient margin/capital to cover losses in a worst-case scenario. Nicholas Leeson of Barings was allowed to run up losses that exceeded his bank's entire capital. Most banks have "trading limits": in theory, no one person or trading desk is given so much leeway that their risk-taking might endanger the bank's solvency. It is a sensible rule of thumb that an operation should not take on positions that expose it to the worst possible outcome − that a catastrophic loss might result in ruin. Similarly, an investor should avoid losses that are greater than she can afford. Trading limits based on historical estimates of risk exposure are not adequate.

If we think of the tree-scenario diagram, the analogy would be that we need to prune those branches that have regret that is higher than we can tolerate − we need to insure ourselves against the max-imum regret. Once we have done that, then we can set our risk limits within the remaining scenarios. If we were a bank, for example, then we would have a separate threshold for regret once we had eliminated those exposures that are unacceptable to us. This threshold would be the basis for operating decisions on, say, trading limits.

Lloyd's of London encountered difficulties in the mid-1990s when many of the now-infamous Names were ruined. They had signed up as members of underwriting syndicates in the world's biggest insurance market. Some Names were unlucky in that they were the victims of fraud: they were assigned all the worst risks in the market by insiders who kept the best risks for themselves and a few favoured customers. Many more Names, however, made a disastrous risk-management decision which, with simple tools such as lambda, they might easily have avoided. Using an approach based on regret and lambda, would-be Names would quickly have seen that they should assign a large value for lambda to the risk of total loss, even if they thought such a loss was unlikely. This simple step might have saved many Names from ruin. But they gave too little weight to the unlimited downside exposure in return for an uncertain annual income. While markets prospered, the downside risk barely registered, and the cheques flowed in with soothing regularity. But its life-destroying effects became all too evident when Lloyd's ran into problems, some self-inflicted, others caused by the normal cyclical changes in the insurance industry.

A technique such as applying lambda makes it clear that, under the market structure as it then existed, the role of a Name at Lloyd's was only for those with very large liquid assets who could afford to pay out hefty cash sums when required to do so. In fact, some very wealthy investors were also caught out by Lloyd's, so large was the cash required to cover its multi-billion-dollar losses. Aristocrats dislike having to sell the family castle in order to raise cash, even though, unlike the rest of us, they might not be ruined by the act!

The same thinking applies to a decision most of us face at one time or other: should we buy a house? Plenty of examples show that this decision is fraught with risk. For instance, in 1981 the Toronto housing market was going crazy. Interest rates were 14 per cent, but house prices had been rising steadily for five years and seemed to be accelerating. So one cash-strapped would-be buyer made an apparently rational calculation: borrow a large amount at favourable short-term rates, buy a wreck of a house, renovate it, and either sell it for a profit and repay the loan, or keep the now more valuable house and refinance the loan into a relatively small long-term mortgage. What could go wrong?

Everything, it turned out. First, interest rates jumped to nearly 24 per cent in the space of six months, so borrowed short-term cash suddenly became very expensive. Second, the renovations took longer than planned, so refinancing was not an option. Third, house prices began to tumble, so the expected equity gains did not materialize. In this case, the buyer was bailed out by a family member and was able to keep the house. But the regret she suffered (not to mention the ulcers) was palpable.

This buyer would have done better if she had examined her assumptions about interest rates and the housing market. If rates rose, it was highly likely that house prices would come off the boil. Moreover, the carrying cost of a big short-term loan would jump. Either or both of these scenarios would be painful. But the pain could instantly have been mitigated. If our buyer had locked in financing at the outset, she would have been largely indifferent to future changes in interest rates. True, falling house prices might have dented her assumptions about when the wreck would be worth $1 million! But she would have had a secure roof over her head and time to spare for renovations.

Now let's move to England in 1989. Our subject is a naturally cautious bank clerk who is keen to move into his own apartment. Again, the housing market is in full bubble mode. Prices are rising effortlessly and quickly. Would-be buyers are desperately competing to buy almost anything on the grounds that it can only be worth more in future. Our clerk could rent a place. But funding a mortgage will be cheaper in the short term thanks to low interest rates. So our clerk opts for independence and decides to enter the market. He has only a small salary, so his ability to borrow is limited. He must put down all of his savings in order to secure a mortgage. For the equivalent of $75,000 he buys a studio apartment in a thoroughly unfashionable London district. After putting $20,000 down, he has to finance a $55,000 mortgage. But he assumes that rising house prices will make the deal look good before long. And even if prices fall a little, the $20,000 deposit looks like a more-than-adequate cushion. What can go wrong?

Everything. As the British economy began to deteriorate in 1990 and 1991, the housing market came sharply off the boil. Prices fell across the board. But they fell especially hard at the bottom of the market. Studio apartments had been created by the thousand by developers with a keen nose for a quick buck. Suddenly there was no demand for them, so the prospective chain of "trading up" simply disappeared. First-time buyers withdrew, fearing that they would instantly lose money in a falling market.

Our conservative clerk was particularly hard hit. At the bottom of the market in 1995 his apartment was valued at around $35,000, $20,000 less than the mortgage. All deposit equity lost, he was forced to approach his mortgage lender. Offered a new and better job in a city in the north of England, he wanted desperately to sell the apartment. But no one was willing to buy what suddenly looked like an overpriced room in a run-down suburb. The only solution was hugely costly. He had to rent out the apartment at a loss in order to take the new job. Eventually he sold the property at a thumping loss, refinanced his remaining mortgage, agreed to pay off an additional personal loan, and finally cleared his debt five years after assuming it.

Such negative equity scared and hurt a generation of British house buyers, many of them young and ill-equipped to bear the financial shock. Indeed, as we write this book, it is remarkable that a new house-price bubble is underway in parts of that country. It is as if those who were so badly burned have forgotten the lesson that prices do not rise forever! But think of our bank clerk. If he had paid the little extra to rent for a while, he would still have his $20,000 savings and might have used this money to fund a more sensible purchase when prices became more affordable. In retrospect, his regret from entering the market was enormous – his financial position literally will never be the same.

Of course, hindsight is everything. There are plenty of cases where people have stayed out of housing markets only to see prices rise anyway. Someone who bought an apartment in New York in 1994, for instance, would have made a fat return in the space of three years. Someone who rented over the same period merely faced escalating rents!

Answer to the framing question: Look at the sentences about our different attitude towards the two mutual funds. They assume that in our brain we have "boxes" or "layers" into which we assign different categories of risk – one box for safety first, another for risky stuff, and so on. Clearly, we would have less regret if a fund we know to be risky were to underperform, than if a fund we thought was safe also turned out to lose money. But, as behavioural economists would jump to point out, by assigning different risks to mental boxes or layers, we risk falling into a classic error: we ignore the portfolio effect of holding sets of funds. This is, by the way, a common mistake among investors. The relationships among the assets we hold (the finance term for this is co-variance) is crucial to our ability to construct efficient portfolios.

Kenneth Fisher, who runs an investment firm in California, has pointed out that the derivation of the term "investment" is the Latin word *vestimentum*, meaning clothes or layers. Investment, then, means covering oneself with layers. Perhaps, in view of our regret analysis, we might consider limiting our "investment" to a particular part of our anatomy!

5

KEEPING UP WITH THE JONESES

I magine you inherit a modest cash sum, say $5,000. What should you do with the money? If you put it in an envelope and hide it under your roof, your cash might be safe, but its value would be eroded by inflation, so you would risk having a smaller amount of real spending power in future. You could deposit your money in the bank, earning a nominal amount of interest that might offset the effects of inflation. Alternatively, you could place the money in a mutual fund and hope to see the capital sum grow much faster than inflation. And if you were really aggressive, you might visit a casino and try to double your money on a single bet at roulette.

How will you think about this decision? For one thing, you will always have a base case in mind – it could be nothing, the bank account, or the mutual fund. That will help to determine how you feel about the alternatives. So, if you choose as your base case the bank account, that will be the benchmark against which you measure the alternatives. By this standard, should you then sneak off to the casino and lose your money, you will have underperformed!

We make comparisons constantly, whether with neighbours, colleagues, or business partners. Often money establishes the benchmark, as when we weigh the price of one thing against the price of another. That is why we go to such trouble to measure inflation and foreign currency rates: we need to know how the value of money is changing before we can use it as a benchmark.

We use many other benchmarks. When we buy a washing machine, money forms one benchmark, but we might also look at consumer surveys that rank machines by their reliability and economy. We also apply aesthetic benchmarks. Some people like colourful carpets that to others are the epitome of vulgar taste. Is your child behaving well? It depends in part on the behaviour permitted in the past, as well as on the context. Fixed rules are one thing, but they are unenforceable if other children are operating under different rules and your child is on a playdate at their house. In this case, the benchmark changes, at least until the child gets home!

How we feel about our experiences may be determined by our highly subjective benchmarks. We might feel let down by one vacation, for instance, because our benchmark is a wonderful, but more expensive, vacation that we took two years earlier. When we sulk because colleagues have been awarded merit increases to their pay, we reject whatever benchmark led our boss to overlook us. When we buy a car, our satisfaction might be lessened if it develops more engine problems than our neighbour's less expensive model.

Cars provide an excellent example of how we use benchmarks in complex ways in everyday life. When we visit a Cadillac dealer, we are there to compare what we see with the cars on display at the rival Lexus dealer. We will almost certainly not compare the Cadillac with a Volkswagen or a Ford Taurus. At a general level, we seek comparable cars and weigh their comparable characteristics.

Then things become a little more complicated. We assess the car's selling points and weigh these in our minds. How fast can it accelerate? What is its fuel consumption? What will its resale value be two years from now? What is its safety record? Will it impress our friends?

More or less consciously, we assign a value to each factor as we assess the car. And we compare this to a notional ideal that is our benchmark. If the Cadillac scores well enough, then we will feel happy about buying it. But if, for instance, it scores poorly because it is relatively slow to accelerate, then we might reject it in favour of a Porsche or a Saab. Of course, different people approach a major purchase, such as a car, in different ways, but it is remarkably common to find a high degree of quantitative analysis in the process. In effect, we construct our own index to use as our benchmark. It is very common for people to use an index of some kind as their benchmark.

Car manufacturers and dealers are well aware of and try to exploit how we use benchmarks. Since the 1980s, Japanese cars, especially Toyotas, have become a widely used benchmark among consumers because they represent a combination of reasonable price and good quality. Now some American firms openly compare their cars with the similar Toyota model. One New York dealer went so far as to place the rival cars side by side, arguing that this is what customers would do in their minds anyway. Advertisers exploit our use of benchmarks in other, more subtle ways. Some people like the idea of owning a best-selling car, so Ford, which dominates the mass market, stresses the popularity of its leading model. Other people, however, would rather walk than drive a Taurus. Their benchmark is a car that stands out from the crowd. Some cars are therefore positioned as quirky. In North America, for instance, advertising for Saab explicitly appeals to the urge to seek an individual identity. Potential buyers are advised to "find your own road."

Advertising in general has two objectives. The chief one is to establish products and services as benchmarks, so that consumers mentally use them as the basis for comparison. But another important objective is to alter people's risk-adjusted calculations, either by increasing their sense of upside ("You will be a better person if you drink this cola or buy mutual funds through this broker") or by decreasing their sense of regret ("Buy SunAmerica's retirement plan and you will have a more secure old age"). If an advertiser can tweak our attitude sufficiently, it can alter our risk-adjusted view so that we will do something we otherwise would not.

By becoming an accepted benchmark, a product such as a car can acquire a potent market position. The same is true of many consumer goods; think of how many millions are spent promoting brands of all kinds. Not that any product's benchmark status goes unchallenged. At the very least, other firms can use a rival's benchmark to pitch prices that appeal to consumers: why buy the leading brand when you can buy brand X for half the price?

If we fail to choose the right benchmarks, we will continually be puzzled and disappointed by our performance and experience. If we live in London, there is little point in comparing the price of our house to house prices in Tokyo. The appropriate benchmark is the relative performance of other houses in our neighbourhood and of houses in other neighbourhoods. If our house is keeping pace, then we are performing in line with our benchmark. But our circumstances might change. If we considered moving to the countryside because our house had sharply increased in value relative to country houses, then we would change our benchmark to reflect our new focus. And if our company asked us to relocate to Tokyo then we would acquire a valid interest in apartment prices there. We would change our benchmark to reflect our scenarios.

Similarly, if we are running a dry cleaning company in Toronto, we will set our benchmark for staff salaries according to local rates. We don't care that New York dry cleaners earn three times as much because most of our workers are not in a position to move there. If we are running a software firm, however, our benchmark cannot focus purely on local factors. It needs to incorporate a weighting that recognizes a going rate for top programmers wherever they are. Otherwise we run the risk of losing our best employees. This is true in any business where skills are easily transferable.

If we set the wrong benchmark then we will behave foolishly. A manufacturing firm might build a factory in the riskier of two new markets if its benchmark was the return it might otherwise earn by investing in high-risk shares. With a more appropriate benchmark it might decide to build in the safer market. An oil company would never think twice about sinking another well if its benchmark was the return on cash: the potential returns would always argue in favour of more exploration. A benchmark that is set too high will encourage us to take risks that will lead to regret. But a benchmark set too low is useless because almost anything looks good by comparison.

If this all seems straightforward, perhaps it is. However, it is surprising to find that life and business are riddled with examples of muddle and misunderstanding about benchmarks. Take the problem of measuring mutual funds' performance. Several firms offer rankings that purport to adjust performance for the risk taken by each fund. Perhaps the best known such rankings are the coveted stars awarded by Morningstar – a five-star ranking is almost a guarantee that investors will flock to a fund. Open any day's *Wall Street Journal* and you will see advertisements for top-ranked funds. And if you look carefully, you will see the small print at the bottom of the ads.

Our example is a Franklin growth fund that we have chosen at random from myriad possible examples. The small print is as follows: "Morningstar ratings are calculated from the fund's three-, five- and ten-year average annual returns in excess of 90-day Treasury bill returns with appropriate sales charge adjustments, and a risk factor that reflects fund performance below 90-day T-bill returns." The catch is in the last phrase. Morningstar's benchmark for equity funds' downside risk is three-month government bonds. The reason for the choice is clear: these are meant to approximate the risk-free rate of return. Yet how useful is this? Although there can be long periods when changes in short-term interest rates cause the stock and bond markets to move in the same direction, there can be other periods when this is not the case. Interest rates could be affecting bonds and shares quite differently. But an investor who looks at Morningstar stars for equity funds has no idea that the benchmark may be utterly unhelpful.

Many companies show a basic misunderstanding of benchmarks when they announce that they intend to measure their performance with reference to a so-called "hurdle rate." By this, they mean a rate of return which they hope to make from their ongoing operations and which often is the minimum level required before they will invest in a new project. Often this hurdle rate is chosen arbitrarily. If the current rate of return on treasury bills is 5 per cent, then firms will

announce and stick with a hurdle rate of 8 per cent, arguing that the
3 per cent is the extra reward investors earn for the greater risks inherent in their shares.

There are glaring flaws in this approach. First, many businesses are
cyclical. Their profits swing wildly depending on the economic conditions faced by their industry. It follows that an unchanging benchmark will almost guarantee a misleading picture of how these
businesses have actually performed. If the hurdle rate is 8 per cent and
a paper firm earns 20 per cent, then investors might think that the
firm's managers have done a wonderful job. If that return is earned at
the top of the cycle, however, 8 per cent is a woeful benchmark. It is
possible that the managers have only performed as well as they should
have given the economic conditions. And it is possible that they have
actually underperformed their peers in the industry. Of course, there
might be a rate of return over an entire economic cycle that is a good
measure of a firm's performance. In that case, managers should make
a point of underplaying high returns at the top of the cycle, just as
they often try to downplay low or negative returns when conditions
are less favourable.

What happens if interest rates change? Under one interest-rate scenario, a fixed hurdle rate might look very silly indeed. Under another
scenario, it could appear highly risky.

A sound approach to benchmarks recognizes that, just as a firm's
performance depends upon the scenarios it encounters, so a benchmark's performance is scenario-dependent. A well-chosen benchmark
should be subject to the same or similar scenarios as its point of comparison. In other words, to extend the example above, our paper
firm's earnings will swing in some relationship to the price of its raw
materials. So the gyrations of pulp prices might be an appropriate
benchmark for the firm's gyrating earnings. If the firm chooses to
smooth out some of those gyrations by locking in the prices at which
it buys pulp, then its reference point might still properly be the underlying gyrations. The cost of its intervention would be the cost its
managers incur by departing from the benchmark – when they buy
insurance, they are guaranteeing that their performance will deviate
from that of the benchmark.

A second flaw in the hurdle-rate approach is precisely its lack of scenario-dependency. An 8 per cent rate of return has no intrinsic relationship with the thing it is supposed to be measuring. In the case of a multinational firm, 8 per cent might be the perfect benchmark in a stable and mature economy. But in a volatile and immature economy, it might need a significantly higher benchmark that reflects the different scenarios it faces. People often fail to realize that a benchmark itself captures certain behaviour. If you choose the Standard & Poor's 500 index, then clearly its performance will reflect the aggregate behaviour of its constituent parts. It is an appropriate benchmark if you want to measure how well a broad-based portfolio of large industrial shares has performed, because both have been affected by similar factors. It is a lousy benchmark if you own a portfolio of tax-exempt bonds. It is an appropriate benchmark if it matches your appetite for risk, but a lousy one if you are highly risk-averse.

The idea that benchmarks themselves capture a set of risks may be difficult to grasp, but is quite logical. When we choose a benchmark it is vital that it accurately reflect our risk appetite and our return goals. A central argument of this book is that our choice of benchmark is one of the few things we can actively manage in an uncertain world. When we try to see tomorrow, we need to do so from the correct (and perhaps unique) perspective of a well-chosen benchmark. Otherwise, we are certain to make mistakes.

Our difficulties with benchmarks help to explain an enduring mystery of financial markets. Big pension funds often make a basic risk-management mistake when they appoint fund managers. It is common practice to measure managers' performance against both an index (preferably one that reflects the chosen manager's investment style) and the managers' professional rivals. An entire industry has grown up to track fund managers against indices and one another. Few pension funds have questioned whether these benchmarks make sense. Often, because funds have unique asset-liability profiles, they need highly idiosyncratic benchmarks. One fund might have a lot of current retirees. Its benchmark should reflect that it needs steady cash flows in order to pay the monthly cheques. Another fund might have hundreds of young members whose contributions will not be required to support retirement for several decades. This fund ought to have an entirely different benchmark. Yet both funds probably hire managers whose stated goal is to outperform the S&P 500 index.

In practice, most funds adopt the same benchmarks regardless of their particular requirements. They will not hesitate to sack a manager who underperforms a benchmark, even though the benchmark was set too high. Many mutual fund investors who are seduced by total return performance measures switch out of any fund that underperforms, even though they might be better off sitting tight – and saving on the transaction fees. The fund-management industry is largely structured around measures that make little sense for the vast majority of participants. A better understanding of benchmarks would suggest a quite different structure!

Another demonstration of how benchmarks are influenced by scenarios is to imagine that you are a child in the 1920s and your father acquires your family's first ever car – a Model T Ford. You are then struck by a mysterious illness that puts you to sleep for sixty years. When you wake in the 1980s, the only car you have ever known is that old Ford. It is your benchmark for cars. So when you step into a new car you are astounded by the smoothness of the ride, the stylish body, the amazing speed! In fact, you are driving a Trabant, one of those ugly East German vehicles that briefly became fashionable after the fall of the Berlin Wall, before good taste reasserted itself! To you, any modern car, even a two-stroke smoke-emitting blob, hugely outperforms your benchmark because decades of technology and design have made your benchmark irrelevant.

Faced with changed circumstances like these, the sensible course is to change the benchmark. As soon as you realized that a Trabant is at the extreme low end of modern cars, you would make adjustments accordingly. In other, different circumstances, we would not hesitate to change our benchmark. Suppose you won a lottery and suddenly had more money than you could spend. Your interest might move from $25,000 cars to $80,000 cars in the blink of an eye and the growl of an Alfa Romeo Spider's engine.

The same is true with, say, paintings and other art forms. We set our benchmarks using a combination of aesthetic and economic factors. Indeed, critics play a social function in this respect. By arguing about what is great art and who is the best soprano, critics create benchmarks for future comparison. When we have a little money, we might buy an etching or a limited edition print. Money is a large factor in defining our benchmark. If we set our sights too high, either we will never be satisfied with what we buy or we will spend more money than we can afford on pictures from an expensive gallery – the equivalent of taking too much risk in pursuit of an impossible rate of return. But if we became rich, money would play a sharply reduced role and we might indulge a passion for Rodin sculptures.

Consciously or otherwise, companies and managers everywhere instinctively know that benchmarks are scenario-dependent. Take the fuss in 1997 over the proposed multi-billion-dollar merger of BT and MCI, two giant telecommunications firms joined in a desire to become a single transatlantic monster. When it was announced in November 1996, the then $22 billion deal was heralded as the merger of two confident firms with two mostly satisfied sets of shareholders. Both managements saw great upside from the deal. And both felt that competition in their industry was so intense that there was big potential regret if they didn't merge. Alone, the two companies feared they were too small to survive.

The managers at BT made their offer for MCI using an established benchmark. They had no reason to doubt the scenario under which they were paying full price for a fast-growing and successful firm. Indeed, they gave more weight to the nasty strategic consequences of not merging than they did to the danger of paying too much.

Unfortunately, things changed. While negotiations were underway, it emerged that MCI was not as healthy as its managers had maintained. In fact, its earnings were likely to be far less than expected by BT. As this news hit the market, MCI shares fell sharply. This had the effect of making the previously announced merger price seem far greater.

Under this new scenario, BT had no choice but to alter its benchmark. It had to give a greater weight to the purchase price. It still wanted to merge with MCI, but it faced bigger regret if it paid too much, not least because it could be sued by its own shareholders. Under some pressure, BT renegotiated terms with MCI's managers, extracting a 15 per cent cut in the price. (Subsequently this deal became even more complex – WorldCom emerged late in the day as a rival bidder for MCI, while falls in world share prices complicated negotiations. The would-be merger became a case study of how benchmarks need to be shifted in response to new circumstances, as well as a fine example of how we need to change the scenarios we use to reflect changes in the environment.)

BT is not the only firm that knows how badly things can go wrong when we pick or stick with the wrong benchmarks. Most people have forgotten by now, but as recently as the early 1990s, banks all around the world were in trouble. In the United States, it was feared that the entire financial system was on the brink of collapse. In Europe, leading institutions were humbled by huge losses as they wrote off loans they should never have made. Several large banks did collapse, while others, notably Citicorp in America, Crédit Lyonnais in France, and Barclays in Britain, struggled to survive. It was easy enough to spot the symptoms of trouble: bloated balance sheets were the result of a collective lending binge that placed the emphasis on growth rather than risk.

But what was the cause? In a nutshell, and influenced by one another, banks were looking at the wrong benchmark. They thought that the growth of their lending business was good regardless of who they lent to and that only the biggest lenders would survive the industry's cutthroat competition. So they measured themselves by two main benchmarks: the general rate at which loans were growing, and the specific rates at which rivals were growing. Loan officers found themselves under pressure to bring in new business at almost any cost. Meanwhile, other areas of banking were ignored or accorded secondary status. One foreign-exchange trader recalls with bitterness how in the early 1990s his trading floor would be brought to a halt at least once daily. The traders, who were subjected to strict limits because of the supposed risks of their business, were required to applaud as a proud loan officer marched through the room bearing the latest loan agreement. The bank in question was Bank of New England. It went bust, not thanks to foreign-exchange traders, but thanks to the very loan officers whose performance was compulsorily applauded.

Spread across thousands of banks, the consequences of this behaviour were awful. It was as if banks had forgotten the basic rules of their industry. Leading firms ended up with huge exposures to developers of office buildings. When the buildings could not find tenants, the borrowers could not pay their loans. Banks wrote off billions, all because they had adopted the wrong benchmark.

Choosing the wrong benchmark virtually ensures that bad decisions will follow. When they endorsed loan growth as their benchmark, managers of banks sent a powerful signal to their employees. A loan officer could see tremendous upside from lending more money, and significant regret from being pernickety towards new business. There were no rewards for not lending. From the perspective of banks' shareholders, this was akin to opening a cash faucet and throwing away the plug.

It should come as no surprise that, since their early-1990s debacle, many banks have adopted different benchmarks. Unfortunately, many of them have chosen the hurdle-rate approach, but it is common practice now to measure loan officers' performance not just by the business they bring in but also by the business they turn down. Risk has been factored into the equation.

Bad experiences have changed how other firms choose their benchmarks. Elizabeth Glaeser, a consultant with Deloitte & Touche in New York, tells the story of Texaco and Chevron, two oil firms. In theory they should have similar benchmarks because their businesses are almost identical. In practice, however, there are some apparently baffling differences. Both borrow huge sums to fund their ongoing operations and their search for new oil reserves. But whereas Texaco tries to borrow much of its money over long periods, Chevron tries to keep all of its debt at the shortest possible maturity. At any given time, Chevron thus has an enormous portfolio of what is known as "commercial paper" – these are short-term bills that typically mature and must be repaid three months after they are issued. Chevron is constantly issuing new paper as existing debt matures. While money is plentiful, Chevron's funding costs are cheap, in part because it is not borrowing any one investor's money for very long. By contrast, Texaco has higher funding costs because it tries to lock in investors' cash for five, ten, or even thirty years.

How to explain two such different approaches to borrowing? More to the point, can both be right? The answer to the first question lies in the firms' choice of different benchmarks. The key to understanding Texaco is that the firm went bankrupt in 1987 and was rescued by a costly $3 billion loan that was put together by a group of banks that stood to lose even more if the firm went under. As a result, Texaco's managers acquired first-hand experience of what can happen when a firm is unable to borrow new funds in the open market. Sources of cash tend to disappear if lenders think they might not get their money back, a concern that clearly applies in a bankruptcy. With this direct knowledge of regret in mind, Texaco's benchmark for funding is set less aggressively than that of Chevron and it can justify paying more overall for its funds. Whether they are ignorant of or simply unconcerned about this liquidity risk, Chevron's managers have chosen a benchmark which assumes that the funding they require will always be available.

Individuals also have to be careful about setting the right benchmark. Above we mentioned that in choosing a house it is important to pick a benchmark that is appropriate for the market in which someone is buying. Hence an index of Tokyo house prices is of no use if you are buying in New York. Even if we stick to this observation, we can go wrong. Let's assume we are buying a house in London. It would be a big mistake to pick a $4 million mansion in London's Belgravia or New York's Gramercy Park as our benchmark: most other houses would simply never measure up, so we would feel miserable whatever we bought. But if we decided to buy in Islington, it would also be foolish to take the nicest house in that neighbourhood as our benchmark. We need to adopt a standard relevant to our situation. We might imagine an "average" house and base our comparisons on that, but house-buying can be frustrating precisely because "average" is a somewhat vacuous concept. It is quite difficult to compare a house with a basement to another that has a loft extension, yet we do it all the same, so strong is our need for benchmarks.

Perhaps the ultimate benchmark is the price of money. But this is something that gives economists great trouble. For one thing, it is difficult to measure prices accurately, especially as they change over time. This makes measuring, say, our material progress, devilishly tricky. It might seem easy to measure the price of, say, a ballpoint pen. But suppose a new pen comes along that costs twice as much and lasts four times as long. If it catches on, the price of a pen has doubled, but the price of using it has been halved. If we were trying to measure living standards, the latter measure is the one we should use. In practice it can be extremely difficult to track changes like this. The debate raging in developed economies about the impact of computers on labour productivity is a fine example of the confusion that can be created when new services are introduced and refined. How do we compare the communications services provided by a modern telephone with those of one from the 1950s, for example?

William Nordhaus, an economist at Yale, looked for a service that had changed little despite technological innovations. He lit upon a brilliant idea: why not look at how much it has cost to illuminate the spaces we live in? After all, a Babylonian lamp was used for much the same purpose as a modern electric bulb. With great ingenuity, Mr. Nordhaus collected data on "light services" and their prices through the ages. Among the light sources he examined were burning sticks; fat- and oil-burning lamps; candles (tallow, sperm oil, etc); gas lights of various kinds; kerosene lamps; and the many different kinds of electric light. The unit of measurement for light is a lumen. A single wax candle emits about 13 lumens, while a modern 100-watt lightbulb on 110 volts emits around 1,300.

The results show how easy it is to be fooled by widely accepted benchmarks. In nominal terms the price of 1,000 lumen hours has fallen from about 40 cents in 1800 to about one-tenth of one cent today. Bearing in mind that 40 cents in 1800 is equivalent to more than $4 in today's money, the results are even more startling.

Now compare this to the official benchmarks. The conventional method of statistics-gathering looks at the price of goods that provide light rather than at the price of the light itself. According to conventional statistical theory, the nominal price of light has risen by 180 per cent since 1800! In other words, this benchmark suggests that the price of light in 1800 was four-hundredths of one cent per 1,000 lumen hours – 1,000 times cheaper than the price implied by Mr. Nordhaus's measure. The magnitude of the difference is mostly the result of compounding a small number over 200 years; the annual drift between the two series is less than 4 per cent, but this becomes vast over time. Clearly, we rely on conventional wisdom to our peril. And it is small wonder that we have so much trouble today defining the impact of new technologies on living standards and productivity.

Once we understand benchmarks better, as with other elements of our risk paradigm, we can begin to do some interesting things. We can use benchmarks to ask new questions about what it is we are trying to measure. Central banks that seek price stability generally use inflation as their benchmark for setting interest rates. But what if they are measuring the wrong things? The components that make up the benchmark need careful assembly.

How Banks Use Benchmarks

We can also use the idea of benchmarks to shed light on real risk-management problems that firms face every day. In Chapter 2 we introduced the idea of value-at-risk (VaR). We were not altogether flattering about it, but we cannot deny that VaR has to be taken seriously. Since it was popularized by J.P. Morgan in 1994 with the release of its RiskMetrics software and data, value-at-risk has been broadly sanctioned by regulators as a way for financial institutions to measure "market risk" – the risk attached to price changes in the instruments they hold at any given moment.

We think that VaR can be greatly improved by using benchmarks better. To see this, let's step into the arcane world of finance once more. In an ideal world, a market risk measure should:

- Capture the risk exposure of trading books (that is, the "book" in which all our individual positions are aggregated) when a significant shift in the market occurs.
- Determine the efficiency of these books. (Could the risk in the book be reduced without affecting returns?)
- Account for the differences between markets, such as underlying market volatility, the cost-of-capital, the liquidity risk etc.
- Compare risk across different markets.
- Assist firms in their capital allocation decisions.

All of these characteristics seem straightforward enough – we wouldn't need advanced degrees in finance to make such a list from scratch. But does VaR meet these tests? Can it be used to compare trading books across markets? Is it at all useful as a guide to decisions on how we might allocate our capital to different trading books? Can it be used for strategic planning?

If VaR were used purely to measure market risk, that is, to understand the possible amount a portfolio could lose or gain over some period, then we would give VaR a qualified endorsement. However, we think that some of the methodologies that have been proposed for computing VaR could be poor predictors of a trading book's actual behaviour. And when it comes to strategic risk-management purposes, such as comparing trading desks and capital allocation, then we think VaR is inadequate.

There are three main drawbacks to VaR from a strategic perspective:

- The measure does not permit meaningful comparisons across markets. It therefore fails to meet a basic requirement for a meaningful measure.
- It does not give any information on the risk/reward trade-off in a given market and therefore cannot provide useful input to the

capital allocation process. It gives us no clear idea as to where we should best put our money.

- VaR is potentially misleading for portfolios that contain lots of derivatives with complex payoffs.

To illustrate this first point, imagine a bank that has two trading desks, one for New Zealand equities and the other for U.S. treasury bonds. Assume that both have a VaR of $10 million. What may we infer from this number? Are they both equally risky? Would we allocate the same amount of capital to both?

They are certainly not equally risky. For one thing, liquidity in these two markets is vastly different. The cost-of-capital in each market is likely to be very different. Moreover, if we were to examine some future period, our estimates (which we would use to compute scenarios) for possible future values for liquidity and cost-of-capital would most likely be different again in the two markets. This will be true for almost any measure that could have an effect on the exposure of the two desks, including yields, volatility, assumptions about correlations, etc. The absolute levels of all market risk parameters will differ but, more importantly, their volatility will differ greatly.

Asset managers deal with this problem by measuring performance across markets using benchmarks that reflect the peculiarities of each market. By measuring relative to a benchmark, usually a market index, one measures only the gains or losses of an investment that is "average" for that market.

Some banks argue that benchmarking is not relevant for traders. From the perspective of risk management and the allocation of trading capital, however, it certainly is. In the above example, for each of the two markets there is an (almost) riskless trade that will yield a small but positive return (differing for the two markets). The riskless trade is often a good benchmark. So if our traders do some other trade, we can posit that they are choosing this over the riskless trade. This alternative trade will yield an expected return whose value will typically depend on the market scenarios that are likely over the chosen time horizon. We refer to the riskless trade as the benchmark or target portfolio.

In financial trading as in everything else, there are many possible benchmarks. The choice is a function of the institution's appetite for risk. Choosing a benchmark with a very high return will force traders to adopt risky strategies. Ideally, the benchmark should be a good proxy for the market, an "average" trade that could be executed easily. In an equity market we would choose an appropriate equity index. In the U.S. treasury market we might use a three-month T-bill.

We have shown that benchmarks are scenario-dependent, that a natural benchmark in New Zealand, for example, may be more volatile than the corresponding benchmark in the U.S. So the New Zealand benchmark has a VaR that is greater than the VaR of the corresponding benchmark in the U.S. It follows that the logical way to compare traders across disparate markets is to measure their exposure relative to the benchmark. If not, a trader holding a portfolio in New Zealand equities might have a VaR that is the same as a trader holding a U.S. treasury portfolio. Yet the New Zealand trader might be exhibiting very poor performance in his market whereas the U.S. treasury trader could be performing very well in hers.

We need to calculate VaR relative to the appropriate benchmarks and not in the absolute. Instead of simple VaR, we need to measure how much the portfolio varies around a predetermined benchmark. We call this the "benchmark-value-at-risk" or B-VaR. Formally, B-VaR is defined as the value-at-risk of the portfolio consisting of a long position in the original portfolio plus a short position in the benchmark portfolio. B-VaR is not calculated as the difference between the VaR of the portfolio and the VaR of the benchmark!

Naturally, the choice of benchmark is subjective and context-dependent. For most markets and for most banks, however, natural benchmarks exist. They could be market indices, carefully selected portfolios, hurdle rates set as a strategic objective that are reset as circumstances alter, or interest rates such as LIBOR (London Interbank Offered Rate; the rate at which banks lend to each other), with or without spreads added.

This language of benchmarks in finance might seem a little complicated. The important thing to bear in mind is that it helps enormously in all kinds of decisions to identify an appropriate benchmark.

And, as with scenarios, it can make a big difference if we know consciously that we are using a benchmark. We have already shown a couple of examples where understanding that the wrong benchmark was at work throws new light on old problems. Other examples can show how pervasive benchmarks really are.

Take the thorny question of whether firms should hedge some of their risks, using derivatives to lay off exposures. This is hotly debated. Some argue that managers should always use hedging to get rid of risks they either do not understand or feel uncomfortable with. Others argue that in the context of an investor's overall portfolio there are always natural hedges and that a single firm's managers should simply concentrate on running their business. The debate about hedging is usually juxtaposed with the idea of diversification: if you can't hedge a risk away, then you can still reduce it by diversifying into some other uncorrelated risk. Many of the risks that firms can hedge are price risks: exposure to oil and other commodity prices is a good example. Exposure to fluctuations in foreign currencies is another. These are "systematic" risks, and, say fans of hedging, it is perfectly sensible for managers to do away with or to minimize them.

The hedging problem can be helpfully described as a benchmarking issue. Let's look at the case of Merck, an American drug company, famous for having been a pioneer of foreign-exchange hedging. Based in America, land of the dollar, Merck's seventy-odd overseas subsidiaries produce lots of revenues in local currencies. But in the 1980s as the dollar swung up and down, so did the value of Merck's non-American profits. This was a serious problem for Merck's top managers. After a review, they decided that it was imperative to hedge their exposure to exchange-rate fluctuations. Why? After all, on the face of it this meant paying significant amounts in transaction and other costs, and it was open to debate whether there was a tangible economic benefit to the firm. The managers were adamant, however, for a single overwhelming reason. They could not live with the risk that in a given year they might lose money in dollars because of exchange rates to the extent that the firm's efforts in research and development could be compromised. That was territory into which they simply did not wish to travel.

For those Merck managers, the possible interruption of research and development (R&D) was intolerable – their business depends on new products for continued growth. They embraced the dollar level of income necessary to sustain the R&D programme as a benchmark. They might take more or less risk in hedging their foreign income streams, but the base line was the integrity of R&D funding. Viewed in this way, the decision for Merck to hedge makes perfect sense. Regardless of other considerations, shareholders simply could not argue with the implications of the chosen benchmark.

We can add other elements of our risk framework to enrich this picture further. That intolerable risk was an expression of the Merck managers' potential regret. Their risk-adjusted calculation with respect to foreign exchange led them to place great weight on the downside, so they used hedging to insure themselves against the risk up to the point where R&D funding would be secure. Thereafter, they were as happy to self-insure as the next firm. But their chosen benchmark mandated a particular level of hedging because they could not live with the regret of anything less.

Let's now apply this to other firms. Think of any kind of constraint that managers have placed on the firm: it might be no more than 10 per cent of sales to one customer or in one market, or perhaps that after a certain level of exposure a price risk must be hedged. Each of these constraints is, in effect, a benchmark for risk. And each is an expression of the firm's attitude towards regret. One international fund-management firm has a brilliant and mysterious computer model that tries to act as if it were a real person with knowledge of markets and how they work. The model adores risk. If it thinks it is right about something, it is prepared to go all out in pursuit of high returns. But real customers cannot live with the regret of big losses if the model gets it wrong. So the fund managers constrain the model so that it cannot, for instance, place 90 per cent of its money in a single country. Those constraints form the benchmarks against which the model should be measured. From the fund manager's perspective, it is clearly vital that clients understand those benchmarks. Otherwise, there might be big misunderstandings.

Similarly, so long as investors are told about and understand any constraints adopted by a firm's managers, there cannot be much useful argument about whether hedging is appropriate. It is simply a matter of disclosure. Perhaps in future, firms will actually be required by accounting rules to spell out what benchmarks they are using. That way they will minimize the risk that they might mislead investors as to the nature of their businesses.

Think how much better off investors would be if they knew both the benchmarks and scenarios that were being adopted by firms in which they own shares. Today we find out only after things have gone wrong; often months later, when annual reports have been issued. In future, we might take for granted that we know the "bets" our managers are taking and the extent to which they are "insured" against the downside. This would give us a much better basis on which to make forward-looking decisions. It might even help managers, because they can make explicit the benchmarks against which they wish to be compared.

Benchmarks can add to our understanding of how we make contracts with other people: two parties with different benchmarks can rationally reach a deal because the benchmarks inform their risk-adjusted calculations and allow them to place different values on the same price. Benchmarks explain why two firms that in theory should act identically take opposite tacks. With implied views, they add a powerful weapon to the negotiator's arsenal. If you can figure out your opponent's benchmark, you are at least halfway to figuring out how to make your offer look attractive. Finally, benchmarks suggest ways in which firms might rethink how they set performance goals and how they communicate their rationale to investors. Who would have thought that the goal of keeping up with the Joneses could hide such a rich panoply of ideas?

6

PAYING FOR PLAYING

It is important to understand that a risk-aversion constant such as lambda is not some obscure measure that is useful only to financiers. It also works as a way of explaining all kinds of decisions we make as consumers. When we buy insurance, for instance, we are expressing our aversion to risk. But what seems at first a simple transaction can hide complex and subtle information about our view of risk.

Consumers shopping for insurance, for example, face a range of choices. At one extreme, they can opt for the minimum cover required by law (cheap); at the other, they can purchase a policy that covers them for every potential outcome (very expensive). Some people choose the minimum legal coverage because of their own financial situation. For them, the downside if the worst happens is not so bad: they haven't a lot to lose. So it is sometimes the case that those with little money will take risks that others, for whom the downside is greater, will tend to avoid. Most people, however, will choose auto insurance that falls somewhere between the two extremes. Most pick a level of coverage with which they feel comfortable. Many pay a lower premium by accepting a deductible: if they make a claim, they must pay the first $200, say, before they receive money from the insurer. Careful drivers who think they are likely to have few claims will feel comfortable with a larger deductible than someone who regularly has small scrapes because he has poor peripheral vision. Indeed, that person might not want any deductible at all, although his policy will be correspondingly more costly.

The ratio we set between self- and actual insurance is determined by our regret threshold. It is very expensive to buy protection against every eventuality. And, anyway, what most of us really want is protection against the worst outcome – a crash or incident that could lead to bankruptcy. We trade off coverage against lesser disasters because the cost of insuring against them gets progressively higher the more outcomes we try to cover. So, we will accept a $200 deductible because we know that paying even several penalties will not break us financially. But we cannot accept the multimillion-dollar risk that would destroy our lives if it came to pass. In effect, we are assigning a value for lambda that determines how much coverage we feel we need to buy.

Intuitively, we know that the chances of being in a catastrophic crash that wrecks the car and, worse, kills a bystander, are very small. To insure against that outcome ought to be cheap because the insurer will reap many premiums before it has to pay out. But we are willing to pay around $1,000 annually for coverage that ought to cost 50 cents precisely because that outcome is too horrendous to contemplate. Because we set an extremely high value for lambda, we (and millions of fellow consumers) pay way over the odds to lay off that unacceptable exposure. Insurers understand regret!

Now, consider our $200 deductible. By covering ourselves against the worst outcomes, we have reduced our potential regret to a level we can cope with. For a lower up-front payment we can now assume some of the risk that we will face bad, but not disastrous, outcomes. The insurer is sharing the risk with us in return for a reduced premium. If we have a few minor scrapes and bumps, we feel sanguine about paying for the first part of the damage because the bills won't make us bankrupt. In this calculation we are much less risk-averse – in effect, we set a lower value for risk-aversion (lambda) in judging our insurance needs at this level.

Of course, there are endless possible variations on this analysis. We may feel differently about a $500 deductible, for example. When we insure the lives of our family, rather than our car, we also take positions that relate our expectations of risk to our ability to survive financially in the event of a death in the family. When we buy home insurance we weigh up the risk of flood or fire against our ability to start again if we have to. When natural catastrophes occur, such as the floods that devastated parts of Manitoba and the Midwestern United States in 1997, we often look to government to bear some of the costs of the downside. When regret is widespread, affected businesses and individuals don't mind calling on the government for millions of dollars worth of help.

Regret also throws interesting light on an enduring mystery. Many fewer people buy disability insurance than ought to. After all, the odds of a disabling accident or illness affecting us are high enough that most people whose work supports a family should insure against the possibility. Such insurance appears to be expensive. But if people thought about the regret they would experience if they were both physically disabled and financially ruined, then they might think harder about disability insurance. They ought in this case to assign a high value to lambda and be prepared to pay the premiums for peace of mind. Of course, it may not be the cost of the insurance that deters them: people do not like to think about either mortality or disability. In particular, young people, who face the biggest regret from disability because they might live for many years, are understandably reluctant to ponder their own incapacity or demise. The absence of an obvious upside in scenarios that involve disability probably contributes to this widespread reluctance!

The belief that they are invulnerable, and a consequent disinclination to contemplate regret, may help to explain why some college students volunteer to be guinea pigs. In return for modest cash payments they take doses of as yet unlicensed drugs. If they suffer side

effects over the course of the tests, then the manufacturer goes back
to the laboratory and refines its drug. Most middle-aged people with
children would never dream of taking a substance with unknown
effects in return for a few hundred dollars. Yet thousands of young
people give far greater weight to the upside of immediate cash than
to the downside of possible side effects. They have relatively few
responsibilities, and the "work" is less demanding and better paid than
flipping burgers or waiting tables. So this seems like a good risk-
adjusted deal for them.

Arguably they are placing too low a value on regret. We can show
this simply by posing a question: in return for $100, would you take
a pill that in an earlier trial caused 1 in 1,000 people permanently to
lose the use of their left leg? Using our risk-management framework,
the student should ask how much they would pay to insure their left
leg. The answer is almost certainly more than $100 – so this deal sud-
denly makes no sense at all. On a risk-adjusted basis, far fewer people
would volunteer for testing.

In general, if we think an event is unlikely but its consequences
very painful, then we should seek to insure against it. And we should
always be prepared to contemplate extreme scenarios. Let's assume
that we give them very small probabilities. In the unlikely event that
a nasty thing happens, provided our regret is fairly small, the net effect
on our risk-adjusted value will also be small. Including something
extreme won't change the deal much. But if the regret seems big,
then the net effect on our risk-adjusted value is substantial. Indeed,
the extreme scenarios can help us to identify where our regret might
come from.

Of course, it would be wrong to stop students and others from
acting as guinea pigs if they still choose to do so. At some level it is
in society's interest to know that drugs are thoroughly tested before
they are released for general sale. But if people were asked the question using regret analysis to make them more aware of the potential
downside, then the price of human testing might rise significantly.
Drug companies would think this a very bad thing – their profits
would fall. But it might be a step towards solving the problem of
student debt!

The balance of upside (in the form of better treatments and survival rates) and regret (in the form of side effects or exacerbation of
other conditions) neatly explains how many medical decisions are
made. Where an illness is seen as particularly scary or threatening,
society and individuals tend to assign a low lambda to medical decisions. We will tolerate greater risks in the pursuit of an effective treatment. Drug treatments for AIDS and cancer frequently are expensive
both financially and medically. Many AIDS patients take a costly cock-
tail of drugs that would harm a healthy person. The radiotherapy and
drugs used to treat cancer often kill or destroy healthy tissue as they
seek out unhealthy parts. We accept that people undergoing chemo-
therapy may lose their hair and suffer from debilitating illnesses in
addition to their underlying condition. But the upside – a cure or
remission – is seen as worth the regret of the short-term suffering.

Where people suffer from serious conditions, they often have a very
small chance of survival. As a nasty cancer progresses, for instance,
doctors might calculate that a patient has a 1-in-10,000 chance of
making it for more than a few weeks or months. This represents a tiny
chance at the ultimate upside. But doctors often will recommend
treatment regardless, sometimes from fear of lawsuits, sometimes
because they believe the patient has sufficient reserves to face the
downside of further medication. But a patient with an advanced
cancer sometimes makes a different calculation. If there is only a very
slim or no chance of a cure, it can be better for an exhausted patient
to forego treatment because this involves less net suffering. This is
often the case for patients who have endured previous unsuccessful
treatments and who simply cannot face another round.

Medicine can throw up cases of great complexity. Although they
rarely do it consciously, doctors are great users of scenarios and have a
keen sense of the downside. It is standard practice to brief patients on
the possible courses a condition might take and the risks attached to
each one. In the case of a complicated pregnancy, for instance, a couple
might be told that one of two twins has an untreatable condition and
that its continued growth could threaten the viability of the other.
Doctors might present them with several possible courses of action:
do nothing, try to stop the sick twin from growing, or terminate the

entire pregnancy and try again. At present, most couples would find these choices bewildering, and not just because there are deep moral issues involved. Without a risk framework, it is impossible to make a considered choice between such alternatives.

Why do some couples opt for amniocentesis? This is a procedure that violates many of the ordinary rules of medicine. Normally, doctors would go to some lengths to avoid interfering with a developing fetus and its sac. But an amnio involves putting a needle into the pregnant woman's abdomen and drawing off several vials of amniotic fluid, all the while trying not to prick the baby. Even in ideal circumstances, it carries with it a small risk of spontaneous miscarriage. Moreover, couples who accept the procedure do so in the almost certain knowledge that if it reveals a fetus that has a chromosomal disorder such as Down's syndrome then they will terminate the pregnancy. After all, there is little point in undergoing the procedure if you have no intention of acting on the knowledge it will give you.

On the face of it, this is a strange set of decisions. But regret provides an explanation. People make the decision because they cannot accept the regret of being responsible for a handicapped child. It is a very difficult decision. Indeed, some controversial debates have occurred on this subject. In Britain, a few years ago, the son of a former finance minister created a stir when his wife bore a daughter with Down's syndrome. He argued in a newspaper article that the existence of such a lovely child was by itself sufficient evidence that abortion should be outlawed. His high moral tone led to a flood of counterarguments. But a simple observation might have focused the debate in a different direction. He and his family were rich. Although they suffered the same emotional regret as any other family who bears a handicapped child, they were well-equipped financially to care for their daughter.

This base confidence is not widespread. Most people shudder to contemplate the financial burden of providing proper care and schooling for a sick child. It is simply beyond their means. This is not to say that they are incapable of loving a sick child. But when they weigh up the risks of handicap, most people must consider money as well as morals. Even though they might find an abortion morally devastating, their regret is such that they cannot consider otherwise. A sensitive risk-adjusted analysis of such matters leads to two conclusions: that morals cannot be the only consideration in medical decisions; and that people's unique regret factors mean this is an area where governments meddle at their peril.

In a litigious society, doctors order more tests than are required because their regret can be big if they don't – they might be sued by a patient. But where do they draw the line? Most doctors make what amounts to an upside-minus-regret calculation. By doing enough tests to cover most eventualities, doctors reduce their regret to a manageable level – they reduce the risk of being sued. But they also keep the upside: the confidence of their patients and a practice free of unnecessary paperwork. Health care is a politically charged issue in Canada and elsewhere precisely because the cost (read regret) of serious illness or conditions requiring long-term care is so disastrous.

More people are facing serious regret due to the move in several countries towards the privatization of care for the elderly. Families can find to their cost that in order to place a parent or grandparent in a nice old folks home they have to lay out large amounts of cash. Often the relative in question has accumulated sufficient assets to cover her care for a few years, but it is increasingly common for families to find themselves facing an unexpected financial burden at a stage when they are already overburdened.

This can cause serious regret. Just as they should plan financially for their own retirement, many families are finding that they need to put money aside in case they have to fund an aging relative. Or they are having to anticipate when Granny's money will run out and they will begin to take on the cash drain themselves. This can lead to the unfortunate and unhappy situation where loved ones who deserve care and respect are less and less tolerated as their assets dwindle. This can place enormous stress on families. Because many developed countries have aging populations, the care of the elderly might become a much higher profile political issue – more and more ordinary families can expect to be exposed to the regret of insufficient funds.

There are plenty of parallels to retail auto and health insurance in the world of professional banking. Imagine a bank that has a $1 billion trading position in Russian shares. It fears that a market collapse in the next month might wipe out the entire position, an outcome that would force it into bankruptcy. For a bank in this situation, where the allowance made for risk aversion, or lambda, has a high value, financial markets can often make available protection against the losses that would wipe it out (at a price). The bank can reduce its risk of losses to manageable levels.

Many people face an agonizing decision at some point in their business or personal lives: should they go to court to contest a point of law? Filing a lawsuit, or defending against one, is a risk-laden business. The costs (regret) of losing can be enormous. Sometimes these costs are financial. Businesses such as Dow Corning have been bankrupted by the damages awarded against them. On other occasions, the costs can be less tangible but are nonetheless important. In a libel case, for example, where one side is defending its good name, the outcome can have both financial and reputational regret at stake! Of course, lawsuits often involve tremendous potential upside too. Imagine you were suing for patent infringement on a best-selling drug you had invented: you might stand to gain millions in restitution. Or imagine you were suing for compensation for an injury: again, often millions are at stake.

Let's look at Dow Corning in more detail. When a firm sets out to make a device such as a breast implant, the worst case it faces is that people might die because of the device. Clearly this is a serious ramification. If things go wrong, the ensuing lawsuits could drive the firm out of business. Dow Corning faced an extreme scenario with really big regret. And the scenario was a reasonable one – these things can happen. It might have lowered the probability of ruinous lawsuits by taking the time to test and improve the implants and thereby reduce the downside to a sustainable level. But sometimes the lure of immediate upside in the form of faster profits is a fatal distraction. Dow Corning paid the ultimate price.

In the United States (the practice is rare in Canada), lawyers encourage business by sometimes working on a contingency fee basis. The would-be litigant pays nothing if she loses, but gives the lawyers a big percentage of any settlement or award. In effect, the lawyers have insured the plaintiff's downside by writing an expensive premium on their potential upside. People who might otherwise feel that a suit would be too expensive can initiate an action because if they lose they have only minimal regret. If they win, it might dawn on them that their lawyer has done rather well by way of compensation, but most people will accept this cost. Although legal transactions are rarely characterized in such terms, when a plaintiff signs up a lawyer on a contingency fee, he's in effect writing the lawyer a call option on some of the potential upside! Thus have derivatives played their part in encouraging the legendary litigiousness of Americans.

There is an exact parallel to legal contingency fees in investment banking. Known as "range forwards," these derivative instruments are call options in which the buyer pays nothing up front, instead giving up some of the potential upside.

Our concepts of upside and regret, seen through the prism of our risk-aversion constant (lambda), allow us to evaluate legal decisions from an interesting new perspective. It frustrates legal experts that big cases which contain major and interesting points of law are often settled out of court, with the result that points of law remain vague because there is no judgement. But it is easy to see why so many cases of this nature are settled, particularly where they concern battles between businesses that are answerable to shareholders.

Bankers Trust is a leading investment bank and one of America's biggest banks. Based in New York, but with offices around the world, it has long prided itself on fostering a culture of innovation. Indeed, under Charles Sanford, its chairman and chief executive during the 1980s and early 1990s, Bankers Trust was at the crest of a wave of invention that swept across financial markets. It acquired a deserved reputation for being smarter and faster than rivals at finding and applying ways of managing financial risks of all kinds. To do this, it embraced two main ideas. First, derivatives were the key to unlocking a new era in which risks could be bundled and unbundled in any way that suited a particular transaction. Firms and investors could decide precisely how much risk they wished to take and how much they wanted to lay off. Second, this technology was so powerful that no big corporation could afford to ignore it, which in turn implied that the traditional close relationships between firms and old-fashioned banks were bound to break down. The rewards would go to the fastest and most innovative risk managers.

At the apogee of Bankers Trust's success in 1993, Mr. Sanford could proudly announce more than $1 billion of annual profits and some of the highest returns in the banking industry. Then things went horribly wrong. The problems faced by the bank have been written about extensively. For our purposes, the basic details will do. Several of the bank's customers, among them some well-known corporations, were badly burned by transactions that involved complicated and risky bets on movements in interest rates. In retrospect, some of these transactions were bizarre − for very small gains, firms were willing to place huge bets which, when they went wrong, had painful downside costs. In one case, for example, a deal shaved a tiny amount off what it cost a firm to borrow money; but the transaction exposed the firm to large losses if interest rates broke out of their recent pattern.

Why did respected (and respectable) firms embark on such crazy deals? A simple $U - R$ analysis would have told them that they should never have contemplated such large exposures for such minuscule returns. Add an allowance for risk aversion (lambda) into the calculation, and only the most gung-ho risk-seeking firms would ever have signed up on the deals that got Bankers Trust into trouble. And even then, one wonders what shareholders might have had to say had they known that their supposedly transparent and already risky investment was actually hiding far bigger risks that had nothing to do with the firm's reason for existing and their reason for investing. Put another way, if you invest in a leveraged hedge fund you presumably expect your fund manager to take on all kinds of financial risk. If you buy shares in a tractor manufacturer, then you don't expect it to be trading in exotic derivative contracts. If you found out that it was, you might well run for the nearest exit.

One explanation for such crazy behaviour is that many firms at the time were recklessly chasing a chimera. They believed that they could encourage their own staff to improve the firm's financial performance by borrowing money ever more cheaply. This meant that the treasury department, which is responsible for the money coming into and flowing out of a firm's coffers, was often given its own profit incentive. Treasurers were exhorted to lower the firm's overall cost of funds by playing clever, and sometimes sensible enough, games. And they were usually given personal rewards in the form of bonuses if they could show that they had "made money" for the firm. Not surprisingly, many treasurers cared more about rewards than risk: they were predisposed to ignore or downplay regret because institutionally they had clearly defined incentives. They certainly had limited regret compared with the regret faced by their corporation!

Nowhere was this more clearly the case than at Procter & Gamble, a firm that is a world-beater when it comes to diapers, soap powders, and dishwashing liquids but proved itself an ass at financial engineering. P&G had become an aggressive exponent of "profit-centred treasury management," as well as a regular client of Bankers Trust and other big investment banks, notably J.P. Morgan. In 1994, however, it ran into an embarrassing problem. Some of its deals soured when interest rates unexpectedly began rising as the American Federal Reserve Bank tried to dampen the economy. Over the course of the year, the Fed progressively raised rates in a series of small increments. For P&G the damage was done by the first couple of increases. Rather like Robert Citron, Orange County's hapless treasurer, P&G had assumed a single-scenario forecast when it entered many of its deals: rates would not rise. Thanks to the highly leveraged structure of several of its "money-saving" deals, P&G began to rack up painful losses when that optimistic scenario was exposed in all its foolishness. In April, the firm cried foul. Nursing $195 million in losses, P&G refused to pay, alleging that Bankers Trust had misled its staff into buying inappropriate instruments. In October, it sued the bank, claiming that it should not have to pay up its losses and requesting damages.

The case promised judgement on some fascinating issues. For its part, Bankers Trust was in an extremely unusual position. It had to defend itself against a customer that had not paid its bills and was using the courts as a way of exacting revenge for deals gone bad. If a leading bank could not rely on a leading corporation to honour its debts and, worse still, found itself in court defending its very reputation against serious charges, what future American capitalism? The bank could show that P&G had entered willingly into the troublesome deals, that it had done similar deals with other banks, and that it was considered a sophisticated counterparty. Moreover, P&G had spurned the chance to close off its exposures while its losses were still relatively small. Its stubbornness, its insistence on persisting with its outrageous gambles, was to blame for the extent of its losses.

P&G, on the other hand, had to explain to its shareholders why a consumer goods firm was engaging in dangerous financial speculations. Their story was that they didn't know how risky these deals were because dishonest bankers led them down the garden path. The firm ungraciously sacked its treasurer (its chairman later went, too). It became amply clear that P&G's senior managers, including the chairman, had little idea of the scale of the treasury department's risk-taking, which was pretty embarrassing in a supposedly well-run firm. During its litigation against Bankers Trust, P&G was thus in the rare position of being managed by people who made a virtue out of not knowing what they were doing! The company's aggressive legal stance was perhaps not so surprising in the circumstances: attack was the best form of defence.

Both sides, then, had a very strong interest in the outcome of their legal battle. There were fundamental issues of principal at stake. Lawyers were rubbing their hands in anticipation of fascinating and groundbreaking rulings from the bench.

There was no trial. Bankers Trust and P&G settled their case out of court in May 1996, less than a week before the trial was due to begin. Why? Let's look at the case from the perspective of each party.

By 1996 Bankers Trust had suffered enormous harm. It had sacked a couple of staff and reassigned others, and it had also settled several other lawsuits, acts which implicitly admitted that something had been wrong in its sales culture. During pre-trial proceedings, it had been hugely embarrassed when leaked tapes suggested that some of its sales staff had almost enjoyed misleading the bank's customers about the scale of their derivatives losses. These tapes gave the impression that a few of the staff saw themselves in competition with less-then-bright customers and cared little if they came to harm.

Battered, Mr. Sanford had retired as chairman, replaced by Frank Newman, an outsider whose role was clearly to restore Bankers Trust's sullied name.

What was Bankers Trust's upside in the legal battle with P&G? It could win the case, in which event it would stand to collect its $195 million debt, less some rather hefty legal fees. That was no small sum, but it represented a fraction of the amount needed for the bank to return to its glory days. Winning would perhaps have handed the bank some less tangible upside by allowing it to claim that it had been falsely accused by P&G and that it had not deserved all of the reputational damage it had suffered. Moreover, that would have made it difficult for anyone else who had signed a contract to sue the bank – the precedent of a victory for Bankers Trust would have placed the onus on the bank's counterparties to understand and to be responsible for the risks they assumed. (That is why one of P&G's legal strategies was to argue that the disastrous deals had never in fact been proper contracts and should therefore be declared invalid.)

What of the bank's downside? Clearly it had already suffered costly damage. But if it lost the case, there was virtually no limit to the possible damage. It would never collect the $195 million it was owed, but in addition P&G was seeking punitive damages and had cited America's tough racketeering laws, an aggressive move which in theory could triple any damages awarded against the bank. The trial was to be held on P&G's home ground, exposing Bankers Trust to the risk that a sympathetic local jury might find for the "home team." Losing the case could also be the final straw for some of the bank's big investors, several of whom were already impatient for better performance. If they sold, the bank's share price would tumble.

Whichever way it viewed the various scenarios, Bankers Trust should have had an overwhelming desire to settle this case. Its potential regret was far greater than its upside. Add lambda into the equation. Under Mr. Sanford, the bank had embraced modern risk-management techniques. When P&G sued, Mr. Sanford's instincts were to fight back in order to protect his bank's and his own reputation. He believed whole-heartedly in his bank's virtue, as well as in the vision of finance that Bankers Trust had aggressively espoused.

He wanted to make the point that a contract is a contract, and he was prepared to risk further damage in pursuit of what he saw as natural justice. But when he thought the bank had acted wrongly he moved quickly to settle any lawsuits – as he had done in several cases in 1995.

This was not an entirely unreasonable position. Its central assumption was that Bankers Trust had suffered its worst damage in the months after P&G filed its lawsuit. Losing the case would be bad, but not too bad when measured against the potential upside were the bank to win. That turned out to be an incorrect judgement: the bank suffered more and horrible damage when incriminating tapes relating to another client were leaked in 1995. And the drawn-out nature of the fight with P&G kept the bank in the harsh glare of publicity far longer than would have been the case if it had simply settled and carried on with business.

From P&G's perspective, the case had significant upside. If it won, it stood to walk away from $195 million of losses. It could also expect millions more by way of damages. Its downside was $195 million plus a few more millions in legal fees. Moreover, it might suffer reputational harm if its "dumb" defence strategy failed. It is one thing to claim you were ignorant, quite another to have a court find that you were merely reckless and stupid! In general, however, it is easy to see why P&G was disinclined to settle with Bankers Trust, or at least why it played hardball in the few meetings that were held to discuss possible settlements. For instance, P&G was determined not to settle for less than another firm which had squared its difference with Bankers Trust. But it was determined, if possible, not to pay a cent to the bank.

In the weeks before the eventual settlement with P&G, Bankers Trust won a series of key rulings in pre-trial debate. These rulings gave it more confidence even as they altered P&G's stance. For one thing, the trial judge appeared to limit the scope of BT's downside. He suggested that because P&G had wilfully carried on with its disastrous bets even after the bank had warned it that it was losing pots of money, it could not fairly blame Bankers Trust for all of its losses. In effect, while Bankers Trust had made the bed, P&G had turned down the sheets. The judge also wondered why P&G should be entitled to punitive damages, as it had never paid up on its losses. In blunt fashion, he told P&G's lawyers, "The unique aspect of this case is that you haven't paid a red cent."

P&G suddenly faced a different situation. Its legal strategy had assumed that there would be significant upside. Now the judge had capped that upside, and had potentially increased P&G's regret by making it responsible for some of its losses. Small wonder that in the final days before the trial was due to start P&G came to terms with Bankers Trust. The risk-adjusted calculation for both sides was quite clear – there was too much downside for insufficient upside. It was now in both parties' interests to settle. A deal was duly struck.

Upside, regret, and our risk-aversion constant also offer an explanation for why firms sometimes cover up bad news that, in retrospect, they should have released at once. When firms have done something wrong or have discovered a problem that would be embarrassing to them, their instinct is often to pretend that everything is fine, to ignore the problem, and to reject any outside interference. Sometimes a firm's problems are undeniable. Union Carbide was pole-axed in 1984 by the Bhopal chemical disaster, for instance, which killed and maimed thousands of innocent citizens in India. In many other cases, however, firms go to great lengths to deny that anything is wrong, even though they know that they have acted illegally or immorally. Hundreds (or thousands) of firms have knowingly dumped toxic wastes in landfill sites, for instance, saving millions of dollars in clean-up costs for the firms' owners. These were cases where U was greater than R because the firms confidently expected not to be caught or to suffer only minimal sanctions if they were.

Firms misbehave like this because their managers quickly calculate that their upside is significant if they can only get away with fixing the problem before anyone outside the firm notices that something is wrong. For one thing, they are unlikely to face pressure to resign; for another, they might save large sums if they do not have to take responsibility for their misdeeds. During this phase of behaviour, firms are assigning a low value to the risk-aversion constant (lambda). They are risk-takers either because they are gambling on a positive outcome or because they are not considering scenarios under which things could get really bad, hence they underestimate their regret. For the same reason, firms will often cover up information that tends to discredit them, always a risky course. (Think of the high proportion of whistle-blowers who are relatively junior in their organizations. Perhaps they will have less regret than their bosses if their revelations cause damage to the reputation and value of the firm.) Of course, if bad things eventually become public, the firm and its senior managers are exposed to serious regret, at which point the managers stand to lose their jobs anyway. At this stage, firms tend to become highly risk-averse. Their value for lambda climbs sharply because they are now engaged in managing the downside. They can also see close-up the danger of not considering scenarios under which they might suffer worse than they are already suffering.

The allowance made for risk aversion is by no means the end of our risk-management story. Recall that we set out the equation $U - R$ to represent how we can view risk in a way that takes into account the upside as well as regret? That calculation gives us, in effect, a picture of the net performance of a portfolio or investment. It is "net" because we have adjusted our upside to take into account the risks that might lead to regret. In Chapter 7, we will explain how we can measure risk-adjusted performance and why this has often proved to be an elusive notion in the real world.

First, however, let's look at a couple of other examples in which $U - R$ might have played a useful role at the time, but can also offer a convincing explanation after the event. As we write this book, Swiss banks are struggling to recover from a disastrous period during which their role as a conduit for Nazi gold during the Second World War has been investigated and exposed. In fact, there were two strands to their problem. The first stemmed from the fact that they shamelessly benefited from Swiss neutrality. Not only was German gold stored, but also much wealth was passed on to German allies by Swiss banks that were famous for their secrecy and discretion. In addition, however, a second strand was often conflated with the first: it became apparent that Swiss banks were sitting on large amounts of money that belonged to victims of the Nazi Holocaust. Stirred by aggressive politicians in America, relatives of Holocaust victims became much more vocal than they had been in the past about claiming lost inheritances.

This was emotive stuff. If they had thought hard about their down-side at the outset, the banks might quickly have done their best to research and pay up on any valid claims and open their books to inde-pendent outside scrutiny. The prospect of the Jewish victims of Nazi war crimes making headlines because they had been rebuffed yet again by arrogant Swiss banks was not a pleasant one.

Instead the banks embarked on a course of slow self-torture. Their defence against charges of aiding and abetting smugglers of Nazi gold was bluntly and self-righteously to point out that other commercial and central banks were scarcely blameless. This was true. It emerged, for instance, that even such an august institution as the Bank of England was sitting on a fortune in Nazi gold that had been taken in full knowledge of its Allies as retribution at the end of the war. Meanwhile, America's Federal Reserve Bank in New York had melted down Nazi gold bars so that their origins would be disguised. However, for the Swiss banks' critics this was mere fog, a blatant attempt to divert attention from the real issue.

As for the claims of Holocaust victims, the banks argued that there was insufficient documentation to support the case made by claimants. This was exposed as hogwash. Many claimants were able to show how they had systematically been ignored or mistreated since the end of the war. Over a period of months in 1996 the Swiss banks were embarrassed by a series of revelations. The biggest own-goal was scored by Union Bank of Switzerland, which sacked a security guard who had rescued a bundle of old documents from destruction and handed them over to an outside body. Here was the very bank that had denied the existence of such documents furtively and perhaps dis-honestly shredding papers that might have validated survivors' claims.

It took this and other horrors before the banks began to change their tune. But lasting damage had been done: Swiss banking had been synonymous with respect and integrity. Not any longer. How could the banks have been so stupid? Arrogance provides a partial answer. But a more satisfactory response is to challenge their risk-management skills. Had they performed an honest U − R analysis, they would have seen that this was a case in which they stood to lose a great deal but had very little to gain. The amount of money at stake in the form of unclaimed deposits appears to have been relatively small, perhaps a few tens of millions of dollars, depending on how interest for the intervening years is charged. The amount lost by Swiss banks because of their damaged image will probably turn out to very large indeed. Swiss banks have already been excluded from the syndicates that raise money for American cities and states − a move which, if it becomes widespread, could end up costing the banks hundreds of millions of dollars.

In the aftermath of this debacle, the banks gradually changed their position, becoming more open and responsive to pressures from outside. But they did so too late. By the time the allowance they made for risk aversion had adjusted so that they were genuinely risk-averse, their names were mud. It was a classic case of extrapolating past indifference into the future and failing to see tomorrow.

Earlier we mentioned that someone offered a partnership must consider both the rewards and the costs: with a share of a partnership's equity comes an equal share of the liabilities. Clearly, if you thought one of your potential partners was a profligate spendthrift, you might think twice about assuming his liabilities, even if the rewards were tempting.

But what if you were a partner at an established firm and some of your colleagues proposed changing the firm's ownership structure so that it became a public company? How might you make this calculation? That is exactly what happened in 1996 at Goldman, Sachs, one of the world's top investment banks and one of the last remaining partnerships on Wall Street. (The only other one of note is Brown Brothers Harriman, a tiny firm compared to Goldman.) The decision to float the firm as a public company was put to a vote of partners. The idea had the support of some of the firm's senior figures, not least its managing partner, all of whom thought that the interests of the firm would be best served if it could freely raise money in the public equity market. Investment banking had changed from a parochial business that required very little capital to a global one with a voracious appetite for money that was used as a cushion for the in-house risk-taking that had become routine. Goldman had periodically raised capital privately by selling small bits of its equity to one-off investors. But the senior partners thought they needed the greater speed and flexibility offered by being public. Moreover, because they were regularly reporting record earnings it seemed a fine time to sell the firm for a fat price. They could see plenty of upside and very little regret! Small wonder they embarked on a powerful campaign within Goldman to lobby voting partners.

To their amazement and frustration, they lost the vote. They had failed to see that their junior colleagues, each of whom had a vote, would make quite different $U - R$ calculations. The key to understanding this is to know that it takes time for a Goldman partner to accumulate wealth. Each year, provided the firm makes a net profit, a share of the rewards is attributed to each partner. But much of this wealth is not taken as salary but must be retained within the firm as equity. Even after partners retire, they often must wait for years before they can get their hands on their equity in the form of cash. And even though junior partners earn fabulous salaries by most people's standards, they know that even bigger rewards await them.

Now, if Goldman were to go public, the senior partners stood to turn their illiquid equity into a liquid investment that they could then turn into cash by selling. They would be seriously rich. But the junior partners would receive a far smaller number of shares because they had not yet built up much equity. And they foresaw a further problem: in a public market, the value of the firm could be adversely affected by the cashing out of senior partners, something that would then directly affect their wealth. If Goldman remained a partnership, then they would be protected by the rules governing how and when retiring partners can convert their shares into cash. Many of the junior partners were all too conscious that the firm had been enjoying some remarkably fat years, producing profits that were probably not repeatable forever. By the time they were senior partners themselves, they might welcome the cushion that would be there because earnings in good years had been retained. Thus, although there was undoubtedly some upside for them in the event of a flotation, the junior partners could see plenty of regret. Most of them voted against the proposal.

This episode exposed a risk, which had been overlooked by Goldman's senior partners, that a difference in timing of partners' rewards could make it structurally impossible to realize a consensus on going public. The firm was in a curious position. Its oldest and wisest heads thought one course of action was in the firm's best interests, and could also see plenty of personal upside. In their case, any regret lay in their perception of the firm's diminishing ability to compete while it remained a partnership. But the younger and more headstrong group saw only diminished personal upside. They could not look beyond their narrow personal interests to the broader interests of the firm because they felt too much regret in the event that the firm's structure altered.

In fact, the Goldman case was even more complicated than we have shown. The option of floating as a public company carried with it implications for the firm's culture of risk and reward. As a partnership, outrageous rewards accompanied success. Becoming a partner traditionally meant guaranteed financial wealth beyond most people's dreams. So it was no wonder that Goldman had fostered a culture of intense competition. For every new partner, there would be several talented and motivated employees who failed to make the grade, many of whom would subsequently take senior jobs elsewhere. The upside was so tempting that plenty of people were willing to live with the regret of failure, not least because they were well compensated while they tried. Thus, below the junior, most recently elected, partners was a secondary rank that also felt threatened by the proposed flotation. What would happen to their goal of becoming a partner if Goldman no longer had such a rank because it was now public? Surely the huge financial rewards of partnership would be watered down under pressure from external shareholders.

This cadre, those who aspired to partnership in a few year's time, felt surprisingly negative about a flotation. And, in a fascinating way, their attitude strengthened the resolve of junior partners. After all, those partners would do best if Goldman continued to attract the brightest and most talented people, presuming they could turn their skills into profits. If the lack of the partnership incentive encouraged many of the brightest to take their skills elsewhere, then the junior partners' own prospects would be hurt. Suddenly, it no longer seems so strange that Goldman is still a partnership! Indeed, one wonders how Goldman might ever change. Perhaps if the partners' voting structure gave more weight to seniority, so that a twenty-year partner would have, say, five votes for a three-year partner's single vote. Then the interests of the senior partners might hold sway. However, it is difficult to see why the junior partners would ever approve such a change. It would be tantamount to signing away a big chunk of their future upside!

Another example of how risk-adjusted value explains people's behaviour can be drawn from the world of publishing. Think how a publisher goes about rewarding its authors. Should it offer a $1 million advance (we wish!)? If it does, it had better realize significant upside, or it will suffer large regret. Publishers gauge how much they can pay by way of advance by making what amounts to a risk-adjusted calculation. They need to attract and retain authors, so they must be prepared to pay money up front – a premium, if you will. They know that if they pay a specific advance and sell a certain number of copies they will break even. If they should sell many more additional copies they stand to reap a modest return.

But the potential downside is large. Pay too big an advance and the publisher is almost guaranteed to make a loss. Small publishers feel the effects of this problem more acutely than big ones. They have a higher value for lambda, since a single big mistake could wipe them out. Large houses try to create a portfolio of books and authors that diversifies their risk. Where they think a book could become a bestseller they can become surprisingly risk-seeking, often spending large sums on marketing and promotion in order to enhance a book's prospects. But they also make decisions that are difficult to defend using a risk-adjusted analysis. Some first-time commercial novelists, even occasional over-hyped business writers, win huge advances. The publisher thinks that it can see sufficient upside, so is willing to pay a crazy amount for the rights to, say, a book on a hot topic – the Internet or Silicon Valley. A hot manuscript is like a lottery ticket: there is no guarantee of a payoff. But because the publishing house thinks it can use its skill to increase its chances of success, it assigns the manuscript a high market value. Such is the unpredictable nature of readers' tastes that many of the costliest books fail to return publishers' investments. The game goes on because occasional payoffs are spectacular. Think of low-key books such as *Longitude* or *Boom, Bust and Echo*, which have become unexpected hits and made fortunes for their publishers as well as their authors.

We hope it is becoming clear that the combination of upside, regret, and our risk-aversion constant is a powerful arsenal for thinking about decisions and analysing problems. The methodology is interesting because it offers guidance on very specific and somewhat narrow problems – which fund should I buy? – as well as on broad matters of strategy and investing – should we float the firm or settle that lawsuit? The range of examples we have found suggests that our risk-management framework is as flexible as it is helpful.

7

THE RAP TRAP AND EVA-LUATIONS

In Chapter 4 we introduced the risk-aversion constant (lambda) as a measure that helps to capture our changing appetite for risk. To illustrate the idea we showed how we might view three different mutual funds depending upon our tolerance for risk. At present, it seems a distant dream to imagine that we could select real mutual funds in this way. The mutual fund revolution that has swept America and Canada, and is expected to change the structure of savings and investment in Europe and Japan, has been profound, but it has its limits. And one of those limits forms the basis of this chapter: it is nearly impossible to make rational choices between funds based on the information that is publicly available today.

We think that we can begin to meet this need, while using the idea of choosing between funds as the primary example of the next step in our risk-management paradigm. If we are to assess risks meaningfully, then we need a way of adjusting what actually happens for the risk we have taken in order to expose ourselves to that outcome. On the one hand, the goal is a risk-adjusted performance (RAP) measurement — we need a technique that properly accounts for the risks we have taken. On the other hand, to be consistent with our forward-looking view of risk, we also need a way of assessing our likely future risk-adjusted performance. How something performed on a risk-adjusted basis in the past does not tell us all we need to know if we are to make smart choices for tomorrow.

Mutual funds represent an ideal way of exploring these issues. It has become common wisdom these days that mutual funds represent a sensible way to save. Over time they should yield higher returns than the old-style bank accounts in which people used unthinkingly to deposit their money. Moreover, because they pool the money of many investors, funds can efficiently achieve diversification with lower transaction costs. So for most people they are a way of achieving higher returns, while assuming less risk than if they were to hold stocks and bonds directly. This has proved particularly compelling for the cohort of so-called "baby boomers" who are concerned to make adequate provision for their retirement. In their need for high returns they have adopted risk profiles that suggest that they attach a relatively low value to lambda.

The growth of mutual funds has not all been plain sailing. In the mid-1990s, American banks were rapped on the knuckles by regulators when it became apparent that many of the customers to whom they were trying to sell mutual funds believed that their investments would be covered by bank deposit insurance. Even today in many American bank branches, the separation of insured and uninsured areas is less than explicit and many consumers still mistakenly think that investment products they purchase at a bank will be insured. More generally, with stock markets rising and a widespread sense that economic good times can roll on for many years, people don't seem to want to see banner headlines reminding them that mutual funds can actually go down in value. (We will show why that thought should be at the front of peoples' minds.)

Similarly, several big American money market funds that competed heavily for people's short-term assets were embarrassed in 1994 when it emerged that they had been taking inappropriate risks in order to boost their returns. These "funds on steroids" were technically under-water – the value of their assets was less than the notional $1 per share principal amount. Afraid of a mass revolt by consumers, fund-management firms chose to bail out funds that had broken the buck.

Financial risk-taking through mutual funds has become a common pursuit. This has brought great benefits: a generation of investors has found an efficient vehicle in which to ride a great bull market in financial assets. Returns have been far more broadly spread than they would have been in the past. At the same time, changes in welfare and retirement benefit systems are putting greater pressure on individuals to fend for themselves. Many workers can no longer rely on a definite amount when they retire, but must take their chances in so-called "defined contribution" plans. These invest in the markets (often via mutual funds) and deliver an uncertain payoff at the moment of retirement. So how our mutual funds perform is not an academic issue, but one which could define how well or how modestly we will live in retirement. If our funds perform below our expectations, we might be unable to take that cruise to the Caribbean or buy those new titanium golf clubs. When we embrace risk in search of returns, we also expose ourselves to regret if things don't work out.

In the days before the mutual fund boom, funds generally reported their historical total returns and left it to investors to figure out whether they were a good bet. Most investors did not have sufficient information to make a rational decision. Not only are historical total returns inadequate as a guide to the future, but also they tell us nothing about the riskiness of individual funds.

Moreover, there can be significant hidden risks in mutual fund investing. One is simple enough. The last few years have seen a plethora of new funds, many of which attempt a degree of special-ization that would have been unthinkable a few years ago. For instance, American investors can put money in the Pauve Tombstone Fund – an index fund that tracks the nine public firms that are engaged in the business of death, whether through funeral homes and cemetery management, casket and headstone manufacture, or burial insurance. The fund was launched in mid-1997 claiming that its investment style had handily outperformed the Dow Jones Industrial Average and the Standard & Poor's 500 among other leading indices. In fact, the performance numbers used for its promotion were based on a notional index that had been tracked back to 1986 and relied on a six-fold increase in a single stock for much of its impressive record!

Another hidden risk is that funds and their managers are not always what they seem. On the face of it, mutual fund managers should have exactly the same interest as the customers who pay them to manage their money. After all, the better they perform, the more profit they stand to make and the happier their investors will be. Reality is not so simple. One academic study has neatly demonstrated that mutual funds suffer from their own version of "moral hazard," that is, they can be tempted by perverse incentives to act in their own interest at the expense of existing customers' interest.

The key to the moral hazard, as well as to the idea of risk-adjusted performance, is to understand one of the basic elements of modern portfolio theory: the level of absolute return achieved by a fund depends on how much risk it takes. Successful funds grow by performing well, which swells existing assets under management but also helps to attract new investors. The "hottest" funds attract the most new cash. Plenty of academic studies have shown that investors do indeed tend to "chase" performance in this way, even though there is no rational long-term justification for such behaviour.

Because fund companies' rewards are based on how much money they manage, they clearly have a strong incentive to bring in new customers. But what if funds adjust how much risk they take in order to maximize their chances of attracting new cash? This would involve taking more risk if the fund has been underperforming or less risk if a period of outperformance might be jeopardized by a subsequent change of fortune.

The logical point at which to alter a fund's risk profile in either direction would be in the run up to a deadline for performance measurement – a moment that defines the fund's position relative to other funds. September marks the beginning of the final quarter of funds' annual performance marathon.

How might this practice harm existing investors? It is in the investors' interest for the fund to maximize its risk-adjusted returns at all times. A fund that has more than half an eye on attracting new money will make decisions that undermine this approach. Thus, investors might miss out on performance that the fund had chosen to forego because it had previously done well. Alternatively, a fund might assume more risk than its investors are comfortable with – a phenomenon that upset the money market fund industry during 1994 when it emerged that many funds were using risky derivatives to try to boost returns.

Judith Chevalier and Glenn Ellison, economists at the University of Chicago and MIT respectively, looked at a sample of American growth and income equity funds over the period 1982–92 and found that there were indeed such changes in funds' risk-taking. In particular, the period from September to December was characterized by risk-taking that confirms the perverse effects of the incentives described above.

There is not much that mutual fund investors can do to avoid or lessen this moral hazard, apart perhaps from sticking to so-called closed-end funds, which seek simply to grow existing assets. But the study is a reminder that funds are not always the straightforward investment option they might appear to be. It is also a powerful demonstration that the two parties in a contract can have different upside and regret. In the case of the fund manager, the upside from bringing in new money is bigger than the upside from chasing more performance – in this case, the existing returns are seen as sufficient to pull in new investors, so why take more risk? After all, that would only increase the fund manager's regret.

For existing investors, however, upside is simpler. They want the best possible performance as defined by their funds' investment goals. They will suffer from regret if their fund manager becomes risk-averse for his own reasons. And this is not just because they might lose some upside returns. In addition, such a change of behaviour by one fund can have powerful (and largely unseen) effects on the risk profile of their overall portfolio.

Perhaps unsurprisingly, there is growing demand for better ways of measuring how much risk funds are assuming. Early in 1995 the United States Securities and Exchange Commission called for industry comments on how to improve risk disclosure for mutual funds. After much feedback – some 3,600 individual investors responded, while an additional 600 investors were professionally surveyed – SEC chairman Arthur Levitt made the following feeble announcement: "we do not need to mandate a specific risk measure." But he also said that funds should try to be clearer in their marketing literature about their investment style and should show their recent historical performance using a simple bar chart.

The special survey that accompanied the SEC's researches was organized by the Investment Company Institute, the American mutual fund industry's trade body. Like the SEC, the ICI was in the end unconvinced of the need for a risk measure. But in interviews with around 650 investors it made some interesting findings. In particular, it showed that when investors are allowed to talk about risk in their own words, they use language that is eerily reminiscent of our risk paradigm. For instance, the two most common risk characteristics that mutual fund investors mentioned were "loss of money" and "gain relative to chance of loss" – each of these terms sounds like regret or risk-adjusted return by another name (see figure 7.1).

When the interviewees were prompted with a list of risk concepts, nearly one-third of them picked four or more different factors, demonstrating, concluded the ICI, that "risk is a multi-faceted concept." An impressive 57 per cent of the sample defined risk to include the chance of losing some of their original investment (regret), while nearly half were concerned at least to keep pace with inflation (see figure 7.2).

One interpretation of these findings might have been that investor awareness of risk is hopelessly at odds with the marketing strategies of the entire mutual fund industry. While investors worry about risk and the danger of losses, they are constantly bombarded by promotional material implying that their funds can only increase in value. Unfortunately, however, the ICI had a different understanding of its

Recent Buyers' Characterization of Mutual Fund Risk in Their Own Words[*]
(percentage of respondents)

Chance or risk of losing money (net)	51
Loss of original investment	30
Chance of losing money, size of potential loss	20
Losing money in the short term, immediate loss of money	2
Chance of an investment not keeping pace with inflation	1
Chance of making money and chance of losing money (net)	26
Taking risk for a possible gain, potential for higher gains	14
Chance for a gain or a loss	13
Volatility, effects of the market (net)	7
Swings in the value of an investment	6
Market fluctuations, volatility of the stock market	2
Not realizing a return on my investment	6
Stability of the investment or the investment company (net)	3
Financial stability of the sponsoring company	1
Mutual funds safer than other types of investment	1
Mutual funds are not insured investment	1
Not having enough money at the end of the investment horizon to achieve financial goals	2
All investments have risks	6
Other	8

Figure 7.1. Investors instinctively respond to regret. *Number of respondents = 637. Source: ICI*

[*] *All open-ended responses with similar meanings were grouped together. Some respondents indicated more than one characteristic; multiple responses are included. A "net" is an aggregation of subcategories where respondents are only counted once regardless of multiple responses across subcategories.*

Concepts Included in Recent Buyers' Definition of Mutual Fund Risk
(percentage of respondents)

The chance of . . . [a]	
Losing some of the original investment	57
Mutual fund investments not keeping pace with inflation	47
The value of mutual fund investments fluctuating up and down	46
Not having enough money at the end of the investment horizon to achieve goals	40
The income distributed by the fund declining	38
Mutual fund investments not performing as a bank CD	30
Mutual fund investments not performing as well as an index	27
Losing money within the first year	23
Respondents indicating . . .	
One concept	16
Two concepts	29
Three concepts	25
Four or more concepts	30

Figure 7.2. Aspects of regret. *Number of respondents = 648.*
Source: ICI
[a] *Multiple responses included*

research. It took the fact that investors seemed to be aware of risk to mean that there was no need for greater risk disclosure. In particular, it found that because a relatively small number of investors was making use of numerical and technical descriptions of risk, it would be better to stick with simple bar charts showing annual returns.

This, and especially the SEC's unwillingness to adopt an aggressive stance, did not satisfy everybody. In July 1996 a group of leading financial economists met to discuss the issue of risk disclosure by mutual funds. These economists made several important points. First, because it is complicated to calculate the effect of one mutual fund on an investor's overall portfolio, it is indeed unlikely that a single measure of risk will be adequate. For that reason, it is not good enough to review how a fund has performed in the past, even if that review includes how much the fund's returns have varied around its benchmark: "Investors and their advisors need information that can enable them to assess sources of future risk: in many cases history may not be the best guide to the future."

The economists went on to make some familiar, but important, observations about risk. Investors' primary need is "to predict the likely range of a fund's return in the future. The greater is this range, the more risky are a fund's prospects."

Further, "investments in funds are risky because they are exposed to economic forces or factors for which the future is uncertain. Some of these are unique to individual funds, but many are common to many funds. Thus, a U.S. stock fund will typically move to a greater or lesser extent with the overall U.S. stock market. A fund's risk depends on how closely its return is coupled with given indexes, the riskiness of each index, and how closely the indexes tend to move together."

In other words, we need to peer beyond a fund's headline returns to the risk-adjusted details. We also need to view funds in their proper context. As we shall see, there is little point in measuring funds' risk-adjusted performance if we do not also view the wider picture of risk and reward. Observing what we need to do is simple enough; doing it is more complicated.

Complicated, but not impossible. One of the thinkers leading the way in RAP measures is Franco Modigliani, the Nobel prize-winner and a professor emeritus at the Massachusetts Institute of Technology mentioned earlier. Professor Modigliani's granddaughter Leah is a researcher in the equity division at Morgan Stanley Dean Witter, an investment bank. Spurred by her bosses' interest in accounting for risks as well as returns, she has worked with her grandfather on a risk-adjusted measure (informally known as M^2) that allows investors to compare individual funds as well as broader sectors and indices.

Is this obviously a good thing? We think so, even though we have a slightly different approach ourselves. The reason is that existing performance numbers and rankings give investors either a partial or a misleading picture.

It is crazy that this is the case. But it is simple enough to prove. The ICI study showed that three-quarters of its sample relied upon past performance when buying a fund. In 1995-6, three professors at Columbia University interviewed more than 3,000 investors and asked them what factors influenced their choices. Again, the results showed overwhelmingly that they use past performance above all other indicators. On a scale of 1 (lowest) to 5 (highest), for instance, past performance scored 4.62. Fees scored a wimpish 2.28; investment style 1.68; chequing and brokerage services managed 1.38; confidentiality brought up the rear with 1.35.

As a more recent study by a consulting group at Smith Barney, a brokerage firm which subsequently merged with rival Salomon Brothers, noted, investors are presented with a strong message by the fund-management industry and the media: "Choose the best performers." Morningstar, a Chicago-based firm that monitors mutual funds, rates funds on a scale of 1 to 5 using stars. The better a fund has performed, the more stars it is likely to accumulate. And a quick glance at any newspaper's financial pages will show how firms seize on these stars as marketing manna. One research firm calculated that three-quarters of the new money that went into equity mutual funds in early 1996 was invested in funds that had either four or five stars from Morningstar.

The Smith Barney study examined whether fund managers are capable of consistently high performance. It looked at a sample of seventy-two fund managers with ten-year records, tracked their returns over various time horizons, and then ranked them into groups. No matter which time horizon the study used, it found that the top performers in one period were more likely to become duffers in the next period than to repeat their good performance. As the

Manager Rank	*Average Two-Year Annualized Return* Initial Two Years	Subsequent Two Years	*Improvement or Deterioration in Performance*
Top	23.63%	13.89%	−9.73%
2nd	18.01%	15.18%	−2.83%
3rd	14.81%	15.35%	+0.54%
4th	12.47%	15.72%	+3.25%
Bottom	6.95%	17.71%	+10.76%

Figure 7.3. Two-year performance periods of 72 stock investment managers.
Average of returns for managers in each quintile over all two-year periods from
1/1/87 through 12/31/96. Investors who chose to invest in the top-performing fund
over a two-year period (average return of +23.63%) saw the fund drop to +13.89 in
the subsequent period. The moral is either that all funds perform at about the same
level over the long haul or that the smart investor follows the worst-performing fund
because it is highly likely to show the greatest improvement!
Source: Smith Barney

table (see figure 7.3) shows, there was a strong correlation between
underperformance in one period and better performance in the
next. Some of these outcomes are the result of the fund managers'
investment styles: as they go in and out of favour with investors, their
performance is affected. However, the overwhelming conclusion is
that investors who rely on past performance – the majority – are
doing so at their peril.

Fund companies give themselves wide latitude when it comes
to publishing performance figures. Let's look at a real example of
the problem faced by investors. Our unfortunate subject is the
Babson Value Fund, chosen at random from a selection of mutual
fund prospectuses. This fund's prospectus for March 31, 1997, contains a section under the heading "Performance Comparisons" that
speaks volumes about the problems of total return measurements
and the deficiencies of existing rankings. By the way, the fund

specializes in "common stocks considered undervalued." Here is how the section reads:

> In advertisements or in reports to shareholders, the Fund may compare its performance to that of other mutual funds with similar investment objectives and to stock or other relevant indices. For example, it may compare its performance to rankings prepared by Lipper Analytical Services Inc. (Lipper), a widely recognized independent service, which monitors the performance of mutual funds. The Fund may compare its performance to the Standard & Poor's 500 Stock Index (S&P 500), an index of unmanaged groups of common stocks, the Dow Jones Industrial Average, a recognized unmanaged index of common stocks of industrial companies listed on the NYSE, or the Consumer Price Index. Performance information, rankings, ratings, published editorial comments and listings as reported in national financial publications such as *Kiplinger's Personal Finance Magazine, Business Week, Morningstar Mutual Funds, Investor's Business Daily, Institutional Investor, The Wall Street Journal, Mutual Fund Forecaster, No-Load Investor, Money, Forbes, Fortune* and *Barron's* may also be used in comparing performance of the Fund.

The section goes on to name a further fourteen magazines and newsletters that can be cited or used for comparison. When multiplied across the mutual fund industry, this amounts to a performance-measurement farce. Any fund that generates reasonable total returns can expect some publication somewhere to comment on or to rank it so that it appears to be a leader in a crowded field. In the Babson example, the fund manager is also giving itself wide discretion in picking the benchmark against which it might choose to compare performance – the S&P, the Dow, and the CPI. Presumably, it will pick whichever benchmark makes its performance look best.

We hasten to point out that our intention is not to pick on Babson. It is merely an example, and far from the worst we could find, of the way the mutual fund business presently works against the interests of the very investors it relies upon for its profits. It should be obvious from the lengthy list of newsletters and publications that there is no agreed-upon method of ranking funds, whether for risk or anything else. Hence, perhaps, the stubborn persistence of the simplest total return measure as the basis of most performance measurement. The upshot is that funds can make claims that are extremely difficult for investors to unpack.

To confuse the picture, some rankings do attempt to adjust for risk. However, they all offer subjective or unhelpful approaches to risk and prove a poor basis for comparison. Morningstar, for instance, claims that it takes risk into account when it awards its stars. But let's say you are trying to compare two two-star funds. How can you know which one is the better risk-adjusted bet?

The M^2 measure draws on a simple idea that in turn was inspired by the original M&M theorem. Just as firms can alter their debt/equity ratio to adopt a risk profile, so any fund can be levered up or down so that it is equally risky in relation to a chosen benchmark (using volatility as a simple measure of risk, although any risk measure favoured by an investor could be substituted). In other words, risk is not a fixed characteristic of a fund or portfolio, but is something that can be changed using leverage.

This is another simple, but profound, insight. It rests on the notion of "fungibility" – one of those strange financial words; nothing to do with mushrooms, it simply means "exchangeable" or "interchangeable." If something is fungible, in effect it is equivalent to something else. Equivalence and our ability to replicate something form the essence of how we reach a price for things. But this concept also works in another interesting way: for any portfolio, there is an equivalent simpler portfolio that has the same risk-reward characteristics, but which might contain a fraction of the assets or different assets. By exploiting fungibility and equivalence, we can understand and manage our portfolios and assets with far greater precision.

For example, a risky technology mutual fund could be partially sold off in favour of treasury bills until its volatility matches that of a benchmark such as the Standard & Poor's 500 index. A low-risk bond fund would use a margin account (that is, borrowing) to create

Mutual Funds (in order of total return)	10 Year Average Annual Total Return	Risk-Adjusted Return M^2	Risk-Adjusted Rank
Benchmark: S&P 500	15.2	–	–
AIM Constellation	19.2	14.5	4
T. Rowe Price New Horizons	16.3	13.4	6
Fidelity Magellan	16.2	14.9	3
20th Century Vista Investors	15.2	11.9	7
Vanguard Windsor	14.0	13.8	5
Fidelity Puritan	12.5	15.7	2
Income Fund of America	12.2	16.9	1
T-bill	5.6	–	–

Figure 7.4. M^2 analysis of selected mutual funds. Based on quarterly returns over 10 years ending in 1996.
Source: Morgan Stanley. Source for quarterly returns: Morningstar Inc.

overinvestment until it too reached the same level of volatility as the benchmark. Bingo! Then the fund's performance can be measured on a risk-adjusted basis. If the risk-equivalent fund outperforms the benchmark, for instance, then it is an attractive option – it has returned more performance for the same level of risk. And its risk-adjusted performance can be directly compared to that of other funds: it is simply a matter of repeating the leverage calculation for each fund against the benchmark. A simple way to think of the measure is that it captures how efficiently a fund produces its returns. The more efficient a fund, the less risk it needs to take in order to deliver a given level of return. For comparative purposes, a better way to think of the measure is that it ranks funds' returns as if they had all taken the same amount of risk.

The M^2 measure produces startling results. As the table (see figure 7.4) shows, some funds clearly take more risks in order to produce their returns. Fidelity's famous Magellan Fund (now closed to new money) had higher headline return numbers, but risk-sensitive

	Total Returns*	M^2	BW Overall		BW Category
FPA Capital	24.5	14.2	↑	Avg.	Sm. cap value
Heartland	22.0	13.6	↑↑↑	↑↑	Sm. cap value
AIM Aggressive Growth	24.9	13.0	↓	↑↑	Sm. cap growth
PIMCO Adv Opportunity C	21.3	11.5	↓↓	Avg.	Sm. cap growth
American Cent – 20[th]C Giftrust	20.8	10.0	↓↓↓	↓	Sm. cap growth
Russell 2000	15.6	12.4	–	–	–
S&P 500	15.2	15.2	–	–	–

Figure 7.5. Small cap funds versus S&P 500. Business Week *rated both the overall performance, and the performance-within-category, of a number of funds. Three arrows pointing up represent best performances; three pointing down represent worst.*

* *over 5 years*

Sources: Morgan Stanley, Business Week

investors would have had a better time buying the less-hyped Puritan Fund.

The M^2 measure throws interesting light on existing industry rankings that purport to adjust for risk, such as *Business Week*'s annual survey. From a sample of small cap funds, FPA Capital achieved the best risk-adjusted returns and earned more than Heartland's fund in 1996. But its *Business Week* ranking for that year puts it well below its less efficient rival, suggesting that the risk measure being used is not capturing the funds' risk-taking satisfactorily (see figure 7.5).

Applied broadly, investors can use the M^2 technique to select funds that are efficient risk-takers. They can compare benchmarks – in the case above, for instance, the S&P 500 has offered better risk-adjusted returns than the Russell 2000 index of small company shares. That may not surprise many professional investors. But plenty of unsophisticated investors might think mistakenly that small companies always give higher returns because they carry higher risks. There can be periods when that is not true, and we happen to be coming out of one such period. Using a measure such as M^2 might help investors to feel more comfortable. They can deliberately select a relatively risky fund, as opposed to merely guessing as they must today. In other words, even after making an M^2 calculation, an investor might choose that technology fund, but will do so with a clear sense of its relative riskiness to other technology funds as well as to a benchmark.

Unfortunately, however, even M^2 suffers from the significant drawback that it relies on past performance figures. Investors are better off with the measure than without it, but they must hope that funds stick to their established risk-taking habits. If a manager leaves for another fund, or if markets change, then their investments might turn out quite differently. As one leading mutual fund analyst puts it, there is a huge gap between nice theories about performance measurement and the complex realities of the marketplace. Indeed, the one common and honest piece of disclosure in mutual fund marketing literature is that past performance (including risk-adjusted performance) is not a guide to the future!

In most situations in which financial decisions have to be made, the outcomes are typically more complicated than a simple reckoning of an upside or downside will reveal. There are many possible scenarios, some of which will result in gains, some in losses. Still, as we will show, these more complex decisions can be collapsed into a decision involving upside and downside and valued, as we did previously, by comparing the upside to the value of a bet and the downside to the cost of insurance.

Assume we wish to compute a forward-looking measure of risk for a mutual fund. One possible way (by no means the only one) to do this is the following.

Today we know a couple of things about the typical fund. We know its absolute returns. And we can calculate easily enough how volatile it has been against a chosen benchmark such as the S&P 500 index – this measure is known as "beta," and we explained it in Chapter 3. As this entire book argues, however, we need risk-management rules that respond to some basic observations. Risk is a forward-looking concept and it can change. Similarly, a fund's beta can have one value today and a quite different one in future. To see this, we only need to understand that a mutual fund is capable of performing very differently against the same benchmark in the coming six months than in the past six months.

Using the rules of modern finance theory (specifically an approach known as the "capital-asset pricing model"), we would compute the change in value of the fund as beta times the change in index value. For example, say we were looking at an American Mutual Fund that invests in domestic equities. We might then say that the fund's risk is measured by its beta to the S&P index. High betas imply high risk and low betas indicate low risk.

However, in a forward-looking world, betas will not stay the same. After all, we have seen from past experience that betas can change over time as the degree to which the fund outperforms or underperforms the index. Backward-looking measures would take beta to be constant. Forward-looking measures would assume that there are scenarios in which beta could increase in value and other scenarios under which beta would decrease in value.

Similarly, we do not expect the index to stay constant. It will vary too. In some cases there is the possibility that it will lose in value, while in others it will increase in value.

The key to our choice of scenarios is that we take into account all the possible values (even extreme moves) of both beta and the index. To make life simple, we will assume that the only things that affect our fund and the index are the possible ways in which beta could vary and the possible ways in which the index could gain or lose value.

For example, let's assume our fund has a mark-to-market value of 100 today. Furthermore, let's assume its beta with respect to the S&P

Beta	Index Value	Change in Index Value	Change in Fund Value	Probability (%)	Change in Fund minus Change in Index
1.5	80	− 20	− 30	3	− 10
1.5	100	0	0	15	0
1.5	130	30	45	12	15
2.0	80	− 20	− 40	6	− 20
2.0	100	0	0	30	0
2.0	130	30	60	24	30
4.0	80	− 20	− 80	1	− 60
4.0	100	0	0	5	0
4.0	130	30	120	4	90

Figure 7.6. Different outcomes depending upon changes in a fund's beta. This table shows the mark-to-future scenarios and values. The scenarios are combinations of beta and index value.

has been calculated to be 2. In the past we have seen this fund's beta move anywhere between 1.5 and 4. The index, on the other hand, has been as low as 80 over the past year and as high as 130. A set of scenarios might be as shown in figure 7.6.

Using the equation (change in fund value = beta times the change in the index value) we get the table of scenario outcomes as follows.

It helps to rank the outcomes from best to worst, so that we can see just how much returns might vary under different scenarios (see figure 7.7).

Let's interpret these numbers. The worst possible performance of this fund relative to the benchmark is a loss of 60 (i.e., a 60 per cent loss in value relative to the starting value of 100) with a probability of 1 per cent. This is the maximum regret. The best possible performance relative to the benchmark is a gain of 90 (a 90 per cent increase) with a probability of 4 per cent. This is the maximum upside.

How might an investor decide on the basis of these numbers?

Beta	Index Value	Probability (%)	Change in Fund minus Change in Index
4	130	4	90
2	130	24	30
1.5	130	12	15
4	100	5	0
2	100	30	0
1.5	100	15	0
1.5	80	3	− 10
2	80	6	− 20
4	80	1	− 60

Figure 7.7. Ranking the outcomes.

Remember that we have chosen very simple scenarios; in a real test we could choose very complex ones that related to our primary concerns and expectations. Even in this simple case, however, we can notice that the fund is likely to perform well if its relationship to the market stays broadly the same and the market is steady. The fund has a 30 per cent chance of performing in line with the index in that case, but nearly a 1-in-4 chance of outperforming significantly if the market does well.

The utility of these calculations is plain to see. We expect the adoption of forward-looking measures to result in an increased interest by investors in the scenarios used to compute them. We expect to see measures published along with the scenario assumptions that were used to compute them. We also expect to see standard sets of scenarios for mark-to-future calculations being made available commercially. Finally, a possible outgrowth of these measures will be the insurance that investors and fund managers will be able to offer together with the funds. The regret measure is the cost of insuring the downside. We expect to see "insurance" contracts in the form of customized put options being offered to protect all or part of the downside of a fund. For example, an out-of-the-money contract could protect all

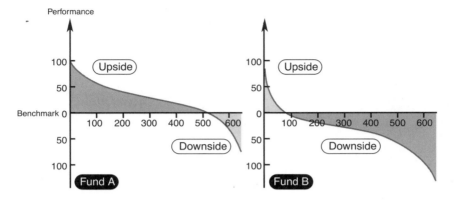

Figure 7.8. Mark-to-future: best and worst mutual funds. These graphs show
how two mutual funds perform in a variety of scenarios. The vertical axis shows the
degree to which each fund either outperforms or underperforms the benchmark. The
horizontal axis represents the scenarios ordered from most to least advantageous.
Several hundred scenarios are taken into account. The shaded areas show the value
of upside and downside. These figures reveal at a glance that Fund A is better than
Fund B because its risk-adjusted return (upside − downside) is better.

downside beyond a 10 per cent drop in value. We also expect to see
call options on funds, which are precisely the forward-looking upside
of the fund. A range-forward contract of the kind we mentioned in
Chapter 5 would give a fraction of the upside of a fund at no premium
and with no downside.

Scenarios are easy to describe and readily understood by all
investors. A forward-looking paradigm eliminates the need for arcane
formulas and risk-measurement methods that nobody without a
Ph.D. can understand. There is no need to fly blind any more! Or,
more precisely, there is no need to ask investors to drive cars that have
only rearview mirrors.

The absence of a "marking-to-future" approach is keenly felt elsewhere. To illustrate this, let's consider the decision we face when we
are thinking about whether to buy a house and how we should
finance the transaction.

Assume you have purchased a $100,000 house and have agreed
to a closing date six months from now. Interest rates are currently

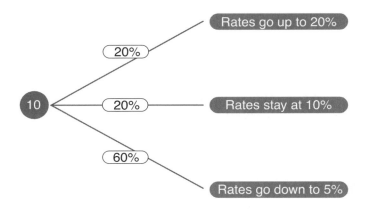

Figure 7.9. Scenario diagram (I) for financing your house purchase over a six-month period.

10 per cent and your bank is prepared to guarantee you a mortgage at 12 per cent per annum starting at the closing date if you commit to a deal. The $12,000 per annum charge, if you accept their offer, is just about what you can afford with your current salary. Interest rates have been dropping for the past few months and there is a chance they could drop further – at least, that's what many market analysts are predicting. Clearly, if they drop further, your mortgage costs would be lower if you waited to finance.

There is always the chance that the analysts are wrong and rates will rise, in which case you could pay a higher rate when you finance in six months' time. You think that there is a 60 per cent chance interest rates will fall to 5 per cent in six months, a 20 per cent chance they will remain the same, and a 20 per cent chance they will rise to 20 per cent (see figure 7.9).

The way to evaluate this decision is to determine the consequences of these alternatives. Under alternative one (commit to financing now), your cost in six months' time will be 12 per cent of $100,000, that is, $12,000 per annum. This is true regardless of what happens to interest rates. There is no risk in this strategy. Alternative two (finance later) carries some risk, but could result in a much lower finance cost if the analysts are correct. Under alternative two, if rates go up, your

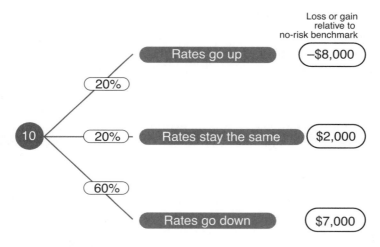

Figure 7.10. Scenario diagram (II) for financing your house purchase over a six-month period. This shows the loss or gain relative to a no-risk benchmark.

annual mortgage could be as high as $20,000. If they stay the same, your costs would be $10,000 per annum. If rates go down, the annual cost could be as low as $5,000!

Relative to alternative one (accepting the bank's offer), your situation would be an $8,000 loss if rates went up ($12,000 − $20,000). If rates stayed the same, you would gain $2,000 per annum since you would be able to finance at $10,000, but you would have paid $12,000 per annum if you had accepted the bank's offer today. If rates went down, however, you would gain $7,000 per annum over the bank's offer (see figure 7.10).

Should you wait to finance the mortgage?

In this case there are three possible scenarios, two under which you gain and one under which you lose. There is a total of an 80 per cent chance that you will gain between $2,000 and $7,000 and a 20 per cent chance that you will lose $8,000. On average the gain would be $5,750 with an 80 per cent likelihood. To see this, notice that we gain either $7,000 with a 60 per cent probability or $2,000 with a 20 per cent probability. This averages out to $5,750 since, when we gain, three-quarters of the time it will be $7,000 and one-quarter of the time it will be $2,000.

So, following the method we described in Chapter 6, if the risk-adjusted value of this deal is positive, we should wait and not take up the bank's offer. Remember that we are calculating all figures relative to the alternative of accepting the bank's offer to lock in a financing rate today. The risk-adjusted value would be the difference between what we would pay for a bet to win $5,750 with 80 per cent certainty and the amount we would pay to insure a loss of $8,000 that could occur with 20 per cent certainty. A person who would pay more for the bet than the cost of insuring it should not accept the bank's offer, but rather should take their chances.

Another, however, might feel differently about the same problem, especially if a $20,000 per annum mortgage is far more than they can afford. What if, for example, the extra $8,000 per annum they would have to pay would force them to sell the house? To insure against such a loss they might be willing to accept a much higher premium than the first person would. Their risk-adjusted value would then be negative and so they would prefer the alternative of sure rates today.

So, even though this deal involved more than two scenarios, we were able to reduce the problem to one of choosing between an upside and a downside. This same analysis could have been applied to many more scenarios. It is always possible to reduce the analysis to an upside and a downside. The only controversial part of this analysis is the way in which we averaged across the two scenarios in which there was upside. Some people might have preferred conceiving of the upside as the chance of winning between $2,000 and $7,000 with 80 per cent certainty. This way it would not be an approximation. Either way, the analysis does not change.

In general, the uncertainty about the future period over which risk is to be measured can be expressed in terms of scenarios. Scenarios can become quite complex. For example, in the above case, we should also take into account the possible changes in the price of housing and not only in the level of interest rates. As an example, we could have considered scenarios to be a combination of an interest-rate level and house-price level. Assume the price of the house after six months could have been $100,000 with a probability of 50 per cent, $120,000

Figure 7.11. Complex scenarios. *This tree shows a combination of housing prices (three scenarios: $70,000, $100,000, and $120,000) and interest rates (also three scenarios: 20 per cent, 10 per cent, and 5 per cent). Point B occurs, for example, when a $70,000 purchase price coincides with a 5 per cent interest rate.*

with a probability of 30 per cent, and $70,000 with a probability of 20 per cent. There would then be nine scenarios altogether, which would be all possible combinations of interest-rate levels and house-price levels. They are shown in figure 7.11. For example, the first scenario is a house price of $70,000 coupled with an interest rate of 20 per cent at the end of six months. The second scenario is a house price of $100,000 coupled with an interest rate of 10 per cent at the end of six months. The last scenario is a house price of $120,000 coupled with an interest rate of 5 per cent at the end of six months.

Any amount of complexity is possible. The important point, however, is that the analysis remains the same. There are always scenarios with final values that are positive and ones with final values that are negative. If not, it is likely that our scenarios don't reflect the full range of possible outcomes. Once these values have been calculated, we can reduce the problem to an upside and a downside. We value the upside and downside separately and compute a risk-adjusted value. If it is positive, the deal makes economic sense.

Although these examples might seem simple and contrived, they are very close to real-world situations in which, if only risk-adjusted valuation had been used, some large firms would not have faded or disappeared. A telling case is Apple Computer: think how different its fortunes might have been if it had worked with firms that wished to "clone" its machines. Instead, since the mid-1980s it has suffered a protracted decline, overtaken by less user-friendly but more commercially savvy rivals.

Another case where a "marking-to-future" approach offers insight is the long-standing problem of measuring how well a firm's managers are performing. With help from a lot of highly paid management consultants, this has become a hot issue. Given how generously many chief executives and chairmen are rewarded these days, perhaps this is not surprising. But it is curious that such a simple problem has generated so much hot air.

Some of that warm draft has been felt by Siemens, a German high-tech manufacturing firm. In October 1997 it adopted a measurement fad known as "Economic Value Added" (EVA), thereby joining a group of big international pioneers that includes Coca-Cola, Procter & Gamble, and Monsanto. EVA is one of several popular "performance metrics," as management consultants call them. The idea is to measure how much value a firm has created or destroyed. Putting the idea into practice is devilishly difficult.

The principles behind EVA seem sensible enough. They start with investors' need for a benchmark. Assume a company is using $1 billion of capital to fund its operations and factories. Investors in the company's shares can only judge how well they are doing by comparing their returns from dividends and capital gains with what they might have earned in an alternative investment. In other words, they could have put their money somewhere else and, for a similar amount of risk, earned more. EVA takes this idea and extends it from an overall measure of performance to everything a firm does.

Thus, for example, EVA deducts from a firm's net operating profits a charge for the amount of capital it has used. If the result is positive, then the firm is deemed to have created "value"; if negative, then the firm is tarred as a "value destroyer." (Presumably its managers then hang their heads in shame and voluntarily give up their stock options!) If a firm can calculate a capital charge for each of its operating units, it can also assign them an EVA number. Thus a division which in one year uses $100 million of capital at a cost of 10 per cent will have to make a return of more than $10 million if it is to generate a positive EVA. If it earns $50 million that year, then its EVA will be $40 million. Thus, the cost of capital is used as a benchmark.

Real-life EVA calculations get more complicated because firms' published accounts have to be revised before any meaningful numbers can be crunched. The example in the table (see figure 7.12) shows how South African Breweries measures up under EVA. Let's examine how these results were calculated. The method for this belongs to Stern Stewart, a leading consulting firm in the field that has trademarked EVA in several countries and gone so far as to register the term "EVAngelist."

The first step is to measure the firm's "economic capital" – the stock of capital it is using directly or indirectly, including amounts that have been spent in the expectation that they will earn money in the future. Then the firm's after-tax profits are totted up. The third step is to work out the cost of the firm's capital. Its debt costs are easy enough: the average rate of interest on its overall debt gives a useful figure. But how to calculate its cost of equity? Stern Stewart uses modern finance theory to assign a cost. In simple terms, it looks at how relatively risky a firm's shares are to the market in which they trade. If they are a lot riskier, then the cost of equity is correspondingly higher. In this case, South African Breweries' cost of equity comes out at 20.4 per cent. The weighted average of the cost of its equity and debt capital turns out to be 17.5 per cent. The final step is to run the EVA formula. On this basis, South African Breweries should have a satisfied bunch of shareholders – it produced 350 million rand of EVA in 1996.

We have taken so much trouble to explain EVA because we think it

	1996, rand, m
1. *Economic capital* =	
Shareholders' equity	5,799
+ goodwill written off	1,521
+ capitalized cumulative unusual loss	930
+ deferred tax	405
+ minority interests	2,352
+ total debt	4,415
	15,422
2. *Net operating profit after tax (NOPAT)* =	
Operating profit	4,306
+ interest expense	689
− unusual gain	68
− taxes	978
	3,049
3. *Weighted average cost of capital (WACC)*	
Cost of equity	20.4%
Cost of debt	10.7%
WACC =	17.5%
4. *EVA = NOPAT − (capital x WACC)*	
= 3,049 − (15,422 x 17.5%) =	350M

Figure 7.12. South African Breweries Forecast Balance Sheet.
Source: The Economist

is symptomatic of the risk-management problems that we are trying
to solve. The underlying point of EVA is to measure how well or badly
a firm's managers have performed. Imagine that the shareholders are
the firm's owners and the managers their appointed guardians of the
firm's assets. The owners want to be sure that the guardians have made
good decisions on their behalf and have invested wisely. The guardians want to do their best because they stand to get rewarded, first by
keeping their jobs and second by meeting performance-related bonus

targets. Does EVA tell you whether the managers have done well? Perhaps more to the point, does it give you any idea of how well the managers will do in future?

These are telling questions. In *The Economist*, an article about EVA pointed out that – like so many of the measures we have examined – it is backward-looking. It tells neither owners nor guardians "how their current strategies are likely to affect the future value of their companies." EVA gives little indication of looming problems. Robert Citron, the infamous treasurer of Orange County, produced twelve years' worth of superb EVA. But a single bad year cost him his job and the county a fortune. Clearly, EVA has severe limitations as a risk-adjusted way of viewing decisions.

But there is also a fundamental problem with a central step in EVA. When the cost of capital is measured, it locks in a view of managers' performance that tells us very little about their skill. In effect, the cost-of-capital number that is generated today becomes a single scenario for measuring performance or for evaluating a deal tomorrow. Under that scenario, a firm's managers might decide not to invest in a new factory because the projected EVA looks inadequate. But they might make an alternative investment. Indeed, let's assume for a moment that they made a risk-adjusted decision of the kind we have advocated. We cannot expect to win every time and, in this case, our managers are unlucky and their deal goes sour. If they use EVA, the firm's owners might be shocked – their guardians' performance would look terrible. But the guardians didn't really make a bad decision. They weighed the upside and their potential regret and judged a deal worth doing given their risk profile.

Let's look again at that cost of capital calculation. Does it really make sense to base the firm's debt costs on its average interest rate today? If a portion of its debt is set at floating interest rates, then its true costs can fluctuate wildly, especially if it is operating in volatile economies that are subject to significant swings in rates. If we think forward, there might be scenarios under which the real cost of debt could be anything from 12 per cent to 25 per cent. If this variability were taken into account, then the firm's EVA numbers would change dramatically. Just take, in the example cited, the tremendous volatility in South African interest rates and the uncertainty in these rates generated by the political turmoil in that country.

We think the problem with EVA and other measures that track corporate managers' performance is similar to the mutual fund issue with which we began this chapter. Instead of marking values to market and producing a single number today, we should mark values to tomorrow – marking-to-future, as we call it. Using our tree diagram, most deals and decisions can be marked to future. Managers and investors alike can them make proper risk-adjusted calculations.

Let's look again at the numbers we showed for South African Breweries. Imagine another company called South African Breweries II (SAB II). In 1996, then, SAB II produced 350 million rand of EVA. If you were an investor, you might be sufficiently impressed to buy its shares. But you would be making a huge mistake.

Unknown to you, SAB II has been the beneficiary of something done by a clever manager fourteen years ago. He saw an opportunity to make a huge bond issue when interest rates were very low. Ever since, the company has had a very low average cost of debt. But the bond issue is about to mature. SAB II will have to refinance in today's much higher interest-rate environment. Moreover, there is a danger that interest rates in South Africa might shoot up in the event of some political calamity. What could happen to SAB II's EVA?

Here are two simple scenarios. Assume current interest rates in South Africa are 15.6 per cent. In the first scenario, let's assume that things are rosy and that interest rates a year hence will have fallen slightly to 14 per cent. This lowers both debt and equity costs and is great news for SAB II: it is able to refinance its debt efficiently, so that its weighted cost of capital (WACC) falls to 16.9 per cent. As the table (see figure 7.13) shows, under this scenario, SAB II's EVA rises to 443 million rand, a healthy gain over the year just past.

In the second scenario, however, South Africa suffers a major setback. Rates rise to 25 per cent, so that even with its best efforts at refinancing, SAB II finds that its WACC jumps to 21 per cent. Now look at its EVA – it has not so much collapsed as disappeared (see figure 7.14). Under this scenario, SAB II will destroy value worth 189 million rand.

	rand, m
1. Economic capital =	
Shareholders' equity	5,799
+ goodwill written off	1,521
+ capitalized cumulative unusual loss	930
+ deferred tax	405
+ minority interests	2,352
+ total debt	4,415
	15,422
2. Net operating profit after tax (NOPAT) =	
Operating profit	4,306
+ interest expense	689
− unusual gain	68
− taxes	978
	3,049
3. Weighted average cost of capital (WACC)	
Cost of equity	19.2% ◄
Cost of debt	10.1% ◄
WACC =	16.9% ◄
4. EVA = NOPAT − (capital x WACC)	
= 3,049 − (15,422 x 16.9%) =	443M ◄

Figure 7.13. South African Breweries Balance Sheet Under Scenario I. *Interest rates are at 14 per cent.*

Now let's analyse this using upside and regret. Assume we think there is a 70 per cent chance that the benign scenario will occur. The decision tree is shown in figure 7.15.

Our upside is easy enough to calculate – it is a 93 million rand increase over 350 million rand. But look at our regret: it is an enormous 539 million rand. We might conclude that SAB II faces a big risk in future, thanks mainly to the structure of its balance sheet. If rates rise sharply, it will suffer a serious drop in performance that will have little to do with the operating skills of its managers. In fact, those

	rand, m
1. *Economic capital* =	
Shareholders' equity	5,799
+ goodwill written off	1,521
+ capitalized cumulative unusual loss	930
+ deferred tax	405
+ minority interests	2,352
+ total debt	4,415
	15,422
2. *Net operating profit after tax (NOPAT)* =	
Operating profit	4,306
+ interest expense	689
− unusual gain	68
− taxes	978
	3,049
3. *Weighted average cost of capital (WACC)*	
Cost of equity	23.0% ◄
Cost of debt	15.0% ◄
WACC =	21.0% ◄
4. *EVA = NOPAT − (capital x WACC)*	
= 3,049 − (15,422 x 21.0%) =	−189M ◄

Figure 7.14. South African Breweries Balance Sheet Under Scenario II.
Interest rates rise to 25 per cent.

managers might use our framework to ask themselves whether they should insure against the downside risk, perhaps by buying options that will pay off in the event of a big rise in rates. As for investors, a risk-adjusted forward-looking view of the firm might put off all but the most optimistic.

Again, our example is simplified. We have made several assumptions about the effects of altered rates on SAB II's finances, and we have used just two scenarios. But the central point is that EVA tells us

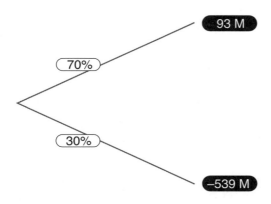

Figure 7.15. Mark-to-future for South African Breweries' EVA (Economic Value Added). The expected EVA today is 350 million rand. It could go up to 443 million under scenario I, giving an upside of 93 million, or it could go down to −189 million under scenario II, giving a total downside of 539 million (350 + 189).

little or nothing about the future risks faced by this firm, just as total past returns give us no indication of how a mutual fund will perform next year. These are narrow snapshots when what we need is a panoramic view. Put another way, we need to take a forward-looking view, "mark-EVA-to-future," and compute a risk-adjusted EVA (REVA).

8

Of Life, Lotteries, and Stock Options

When one of the authors was a naive college student, he sat drinking coffee with friends one lazy afternoon and encountered an age-old excitement. One of his group remarked that he had just done a clever thing. He had responded to a chain letter and sent about $75 in total to four people named in the letter. In return, his name would feature on the list in the chain, rising to the top after the letter was passed on a few times, at which point he would suddenly be flooded with money worth his $75 many times over. Half of the group's reaction was to laugh. How could our friend have been so silly? Didn't he know that he was unlikely ever to see a penny, that these schemes do the rounds occasionally and rarely benefit more than a tiny number of people? That $75 could have been better used buying a few rounds of drinks in the college bar.

But the other half of the group was intrigued and an earnest, if somewhat greedy, discussion ensued. If this letter had proved so compelling that one of us had actually sent off money, surely there was gold at the end of the rainbow. All we had to do was to start our own letter, thereby ensuring that the early returns would reach us before the thing ran out of steam. Alas, it was not so simple, as we soon discovered. None of us ever saw a penny of return on the idea, including the friend who originated our interest. But several weeks of effort and hope were spent in vain before we learned the truth about Ponzi schemes.

Why do such schemes trap so many and why are they so persistent? The question is important because pyramid investment schemes have been plaguing some countries' efforts to emerge from Communist rule. Romania saw a couple of fantastic schemes in the mid-1990s, schemes that temporarily offered people a quick escape from poverty, only to ruin those who were trapped when the party stopped. In Albania crooked investment schemes were directly implicated in the breakdown of civil order in 1997. So many people had invested in the schemes that the social pain was intolerable when they collapsed. Even when they knew that the schemes were incredibly risky, people went on investing their money, hoping that they would get out before the last and final round.

Ponzi schemes work because they appeal to our sense of upside. They create a false view of positive risk-adjusted return by exaggerating the upside relative to a small, fixed downside. Poor college students and Albanians probably shared the hope that if only they could grasp the promised returns, then their lives would be immeasurably improved. Of course, the loss of $75, though painful, would not be disastrous for most students. But when thousands of people lost everything in Albania, their regret was so high that they took to the streets. It is reckoned that as much as $2 billion was lost in Albania's pyramid schemes, equivalent to around half that country's official gross annual economic output.

In fact, pyramid schemes are not limited to cash rip-offs; they come in many guises. How many of us know friends or family who have been seduced, even if temporarily, into buying expensive stocks of vitamin pills, vacuum cleaners, or cosmetics? The promise is always a variation on the theme that this wonder product, which is usually not

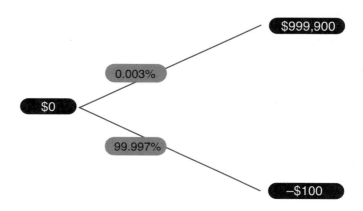

Figure 8.1. Scenario diagram for a Toronto lottery. *This diagram depicts the process of valuing a decision to buy a lottery ticket advertised in a Toronto newspaper. The ticket costs $100 and has a prize of $1 million. The net gain is therefore $999,900. The chances of winning are 1 in 30,000 or 0.003 per cent. Consequently, the chances of losing are 99.997 per cent and the amount we can lose is the price of the ticket.*

available in the shops, will yield wealth and prosperity. A few people, through perseverance and sales ability, work their way to the top of the heap. But the remarkable thing about all of these schemes is that almost all of the benefits accrue to those who initiate and run them. Those lower down the chain are usually working to enrich those at the top. They do it because they put a high weight on the upside. In the case of wonder-product schemes, that upside might be something other than money. Some of the people who get involved may yearn for the independence and freedom of what seems to be self-employment. They value a psychological upside more than the financial regret caused by owning more shampoo than they can ever use.

If pyramid schemes were properly analysed by their potential victims, then most would fail. The same should be true of the many lotteries that offer poor chances of success. The risk-adjusted valuation approach we have developed is a good way of understanding why in some cases we play lotteries, even when the odds are overwhelmingly against us.

As we write this book, in Toronto you can buy a lottery ticket for

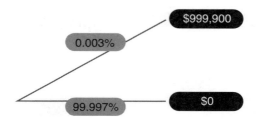

Figure 8.2. Toronto lottery. *The upside is $1 million minus the cost of the ticket.*

$100 that has a prize of $1 million. By law the total number of tickets must be announced in the press. In this case, it is 30,000. Assuming the lottery promoter sells all the tickets, that means there is a 1-in-30,000 chance of winning. Thus the fair or expected value of the ticket should be 1/30,000th of a million dollars or $33. Yet the lottery is greatly over-subscribed, with many mathematicians, teachers, and university professors among those who are buying tickets! Lotteries have been famously described as a "tax on the stupid." How to explain the fact that in this case Ph.D.'s are among the apparently gullible? The answer comes from analysing the example using our risk-adjusted approach.

Using scenario trees to describe the lottery (see figure 8.2), we see that the downside is $100 (the cost of the ticket) and the upside is $999,900 (the net amount you will earn from the lottery, $1,000,000 − $100). We now break the problem up into two decisions: a bet and insurance.

For the bet (the upside), we ask you what is the most you would pay for a very, very small chance of winning almost a million dollars (see figure 8.2). Well, many people would pay more than $100 for such an opportunity.

For the insurance (the downside), we ask you how much you would spend to insure an almost certain loss of $100 (see figure 8.3). Certainly it would be some number less than $100 since you can only lose $100, so why spend $100 or more on insuring the loss?

The risk-adjusted value would then be positive (more than $100 minus some number less than $100, which is positive). Therefore we expect people to play the lottery. Participants are not as stupid as they might seem!

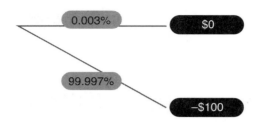

Figure 8.3. Toronto lottery. *The downside is precisely the cost of the ticket.*

The difference between this example and the previous ones is that it shows that sometimes, particularly when the payoffs are large enough and regret is relatively small, people will be prepared to pay much more than the expected value for a bet. In this case they pay $100, far more than the expected value, which is $33. In the first example we agreed that most of us would pay much less than the expected value of $800 to win $1,000 with 80 per cent certainty.

Another interesting aspect of human behaviour in such decisions is what happens when the amounts are changed but the odds aren't. For example, what if the Toronto lottery had the same odds (1 in 30,000) but read "A chance to win $1 billion" (1,000 times more) and the tickets cost $100,000 (also 1,000 times more). There would be far fewer takers for this lottery because the loss of $100,000 would be devastating. The regret in this case is too high.

Another way of expressing this is that we would pay more to insure an almost certain loss of $100,000 (downside insurance) than we would pay for a very small chance of winning a billion dollars (upside value). Certainly very few people would even be able to contemplate spending $33,333 (the expected value), never mind $100,000 (the scaled-up ticket price), for a ticket that has a very small chance of winning, no matter how great the possible reward. Yet for the scaled-down lottery, people were prepared to pay more than the expected value of the bet. As the stakes get very high, the value of the downside outweighs the value of the upside and so the risk-adjusted value is negative.

In many circumstances, investment or other choices involving financial uncertainty involve more than a simple choice between upside

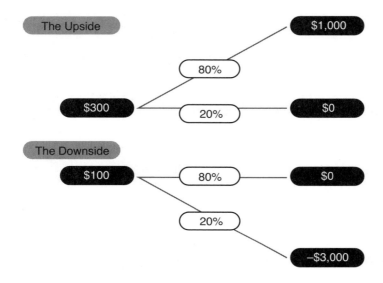

Figure 8.4. Investing $3,000 – the upside and the downside. The upside is what we would pay for the bet to win $1,000. The downside is what we would pay to insure against the loss of $3,000.

and downside. There will be many possible scenarios and hence many possible outcomes. But at the end of the day, all financial-decision problems, as well as many non-financial ones, can be reduced to the risk-adjusted analysis we have demonstrated here.

For each decision we have to make there is an upside and a downside. When the market is incomplete, the values associated with the upside and downside will be subjective. These values determine how the decision-maker discounts future earnings/losses under the upside and downside scenarios. To see this, let's look again at the example we first studied in Chapter 3. You have received a $3,000 gift. Your broker offers to invest it in a fund and she outlines the possibilities as follows. After one month the $3,000 will increase to $4,000 with a likelihood of 80 per cent or will be worth zero with 20 per cent likelihood (see figure 8.4).

Since the future value is $1,000 for the upside and today's value as given by the decision-maker is $300, we can deduce that the discount factor applied to the upside is 300/1,000 or 3/10. In a similar fashion, we can say that the decision-maker has discounted the downside value in the future to get today's value by 100/3,000 or 1/30.

These discount factors are extremely useful if we wish to obtain a risk-adjusted value for a similar problem with future payoffs that are not far different from the ones above. For example, you might ask what the risk-adjusted value would be if the downside future loss was $3,900 and the upside future value was only $500. The downside value would be 1/30 of $3,900, which equals $130. The upside would be 3/10 of $500, which equals $150. So the risk-adjusted value would be $20.

Even more interesting is the view this decision-maker has implied by the valuation she has given. The "implied view" is the set of probabilities and discount rate that we can determine from her valuation of the upside and downside. In this case the discount factors are 3/10 (= 9/30) and 1/30 respectively. Thus her implied view is a probability of 9/10 for the upside and 1/10 for the downside and a discount rate of 1/3 for the period. Note that $(1/3) \times (9/10) = 9/30 = 3/10$ and $(1/3) \times (1/10) = 1/30$, which are the discount factors implied by the decision-maker.

We can interpret this in the following way. The decision-maker has associated an implied probability of 9/10 with the upside event, which exceeds the subjective probability that was associated with the upside. Her implied view is that the upside should be weighted more heavily than indicated and consequently that the downside should be discounted relative to the expected value. Another way of expressing this is that her implied view is "bullish."

This simple observation has enormous implications. It means, for instance, that with limited information we can learn a great deal about a decision-maker and then tailor contracts that are likely to appeal to her. This significantly enhances our negotiating position. At the very least, it means that we can set a range of values beyond which we know that our potential counterparty will not be interested in dealing with us.

The early stages of negotiating usually involve lengthy games as we try to sound out a would-be counterparty or customer. It can be very hard to read people's intentions because we have no way of knowing what they are really thinking. Will they offer a low price, and what would this signal? Is it really an opening bid, or are they serious about walking away if the price is higher? Should we demand a high price at the outset and be prepared to reduce it later? Or should we pitch a realistic price? Or should we try to influence their risk-adjusted value by throwing some "scare" scenarios at them?

This is where implied views can help. In a situation where we are selling something and have six possible buyers, we might ask them to submit preliminary bids based on the same information. In this case, we might ask them to tell us under certain scenarios what they would be prepared to bid. Provided we have framed the bidding request correctly, we might find that we can eliminate four parties simply by taking their bids and calculating their implied views and realizing that they are significantly less bullish than the remaining two. In other words, we would know that these potential buyers are far less likely to bid the biggest price for what we are selling. We can narrow our efforts to the most bullish buyers who are likely to see the highest risk-adjusted value in our product or property. And we can negotiate from a position of relative strength because we are fairly confident that our bullish buyers want to do a deal – they can see positive value in the trade.

Of course, there is nothing stopping buyers from also using the technique. For instance, they could canvass possible suppliers with a request for information about prices and quantities under certain scenarios. Using the information provided, they could calculate the suppliers' implied views and focus their efforts on the two that seem likeliest to want to do a deal.

The fact that someone's implied views can be bullish (or bearish) also lends a clue as to why the combination of upside and regret is a better way of describing people's behaviour than that provided by classical economics. In Chapter 4 we met Microsoft Man. Obviously his implied view was bullish in the extreme – he though Microsoft shares were a one-way bet. Provided he could afford large losses in the event that Microsoft shares were to fall in value, then his behaviour was not necessarily irrational. Now, Microsoft Man has plenty of company, not least among Microsoft employees. Many of them have become extremely rich thanks to the firm's generous attitude towards stock options.

Options have become a standard means for corporations to reward employees because they appear to offer a genuine win–win contract – that is, one in which both sides in the deal think they have a positive risk-adjusted value. To traditional economists this appears puzzling. Surely deals that are properly priced must be win–lose contracts. Certainly someone thinking of granting stock options in his company would do so only if he thought the options would be properly priced. On the other side, employees must often forego salary in order to receive options, something they would be reluctant to do if they thought the options were overpriced. In isolation, based on each side's expected values, it is hard to see how in a world of symmetrical contracts there would be any stock options – the two sides simply could not meet at an agreed price.

The solution to this conundrum is that options can represent win–win contracts in certain circumstances. If we put upside and regret into the equation, it is easy to see that for both sides stock options offer significant upside offset by little regret. For the entrepreneur, options can defer salary costs during a period when the firm desperately needs its cash flow. Alternatively, options can be a way of holding on to valuable staff which the firm could not otherwise afford to keep. Imagine a key member of staff at a small but fast-growing technology firm was offered a fat salary by an established rival. The small firm cannot possibly match the salary offer, not least because it could not afford the precedent among its remaining workers. But it can use options (future returns) as a way of enticing the employee to stay. In effect, the entrepreneur dangles upside to employees whose implied views are sufficiently bullish that they see a positive risk-adjusted value. An employee who chose to leave could indeed incur a great deal of regret if it turned out that the firm was floated on the stock market and went on to perform spectacularly.

Small firms are usually particularly vulnerable to a small number of their top employees. Typically these managers dominate the firm's external contacts – they represent it at sales meetings and trade conferences. And that brings them to the attention of rivals that are always looking for talent. It is common for well-established firms to pitch lucrative offers. If you are currently being paid $60,000 and a few options, and a big firm offers you $400,000 and a guaranteed bonus of $100,000 after one year, then it is a rare person who is not seriously tempted. But if those options are potentially worth $2 million should the firm float in a year's time, then the temptation will be so much smaller.

When a firm is no longer fast-growing, options can become a less attractive form of reward. In the case of Microsoft, for instance, many of its young programmers (the so-called "geeks") became fabulously wealthy thanks to their options. The firm's booming stock price meant that even relatively recent arrivals could accumulate significant wealth. This has left the firm vulnerable to its own staff. Instead of being beholden to the firm, plenty of staff have sufficient wealth that they can walk away. Many have done so, opting to explore the slower-paced world of not-for-profit enterprises or to start the families that they deferred while writing code for Bill Gates.

The rise in the share price also has a paradoxical effect, in that it increases the now-wealthy employees' potential regret. If you own a bunch of options, which have not vested, then your upside is largely theoretical until the moment you can cash them in. But once your options have vested, then you have a real exposure to the firm. Should its share price suddenly collapse, you will experience massive regret. So many Microsoft employees, like Microsoft Man, now face large regret because their wealth is concentrated. Indeed, in some ways the company encourages this. Employees can opt for a number of pension and savings plans that allow them to buy Microsoft shares at a discount. Many staff choose to "save" as much as they can this way because historically such offerings have been so lucrative.

Microsoft's spectacular success has meant that its new employees no longer find options as alluring as their predecessors did. As Microsoft has grown, it has taken on hundreds of staff who do not fit into the geek category. Indeed, thanks to the firm's efforts in an array of businesses, it now has many staff who barely know their way around a PC. These staff approach share options from a new angle. It is highly unlikely that the firm's shares will experience the same upside in the next five years as the last. Consequently, options will prove a significantly less attractive alternative to salary. Many new

Microsoft employees are in mid-career, living in cities such as New York where it costs real money to rent apartments and buy dinner. In theory they might like to forego some salary for options, but in practice, their immediate need for cash prevents them. That can create curious resentments. For instance, a newly appointed senior manager might feel quite peculiar when confronted by a much younger subordinate who happens to be a multimillionaire.

It is hard to overstate the obsession with options among businesses and workers alike. In the United States and Canada, options have become a standard tool in corporate finance. It is reckoned that among America's top 200 firms, options now account for nearly 12 per cent of shares outstanding, compared with less than 7 per cent at the end of the 1980s. Whereas in the mid-1980s the value of shares set aside for options was around $60 billion, these days the number is more like $300 billion.

Fashion-conscious firms abroad have jumped on the bandwagon. You only have to see the fuss over the options-laden pay packets of bosses of privatized water and electrical utilities in Britain to see how far the game has gone. But it is a dangerous game on all sides. Inherent in it is a single scenario – that the share price will rise sufficiently that the options will have value. The benefits to the firm last until options have vested. The benefits to the employee accrue only after options have vested, but then serve to decouple the employee's interests from those of the firm.

Investment banks are plagued by an options-related problem. Each year they award their staff bonuses based upon performance. These payouts are the equivalent of options vesting – during the year, staff in effect have a call option on the firm's upside. The problem for banks is that once bonuses have been paid the staff have no incentive to stay if there is a higher bid for their skills from a rival. No sooner do bankers cash in than many of them check out. Moreover, bonus schemes have caused perverse behaviour. Banks come under great pressure to pay bonuses even when they have not had particularly profitable years. They argue that this is the only way to keep their best people, just as other firms claim that stock options are the only way to keep theirs. In addition, banks have to watch carefully to make sure that their traders are not taking undue risks as they chase the high returns that will bring them life-altering bonuses. In other words, while traders should be encouraged to pursue the upside, the firm should make sure that they are not exposing it to regret. Every deal the bank enters into should make sense on a risk-adjusted basis!

Many investment banks now insist that a chunk of staff bonuses be withheld for a set period, sometimes a year or two, sometimes longer. Instead of being paid all in cash, a portion of bonuses is now paid in the form of shares, a move intended to tie workers to the firm. Anyone who leaves for a rival firm is forced to give up any bonus entitlements. Of course, as one or two banks have found, there can be an occasional opposite effect: deferred compensation can make it more difficult to winkle out employees whose departure would cause no regret!

There have been several cases in the United States where shareholders have revolted after managers voted themselves particularly generous options. And during 1997 there was the beginning of a widespread realization that if options are too rich for managers then the firm can actually suffer harm. If a group of determined managers wished, they could effectively manage the firm to maximize share prices up to the point where options would become hugely valuable. One academic study found that managers who have big dollops of options tend to be keener to make strategic acquisitions and divestitures, as if to justify to shareholders that they are working for their rewards. Another study found that an embarrassing number of firms award stock options to managers just before the firm reports a spree of good news that sends its stock price soaring. In such cases, options cease to be win-win contracts, but rather become instruments by which managers grab value from shareholders.

In response, the best-managed firms are tempering their use of options. In Chapter 7 we mentioned that Monsanto is among those firms that have embraced EVA. It is also a pioneer of stock options for bosses that offer win-win terms to shareholders. Its managers are rewarded in two ways. First, four sets of options are triggered when the share price passes set levels: $150, $175, $200, and $225, against a current share price of around $40. Second, and innovatively, managers are required to purchase shares in Monsanto using money that the company lends to them. Only if they meet some stiff targets – performing better than three-quarters of a group of industrial rivals for a set number of years, for instance – do they keep the shares. Otherwise, they must use their own money to pay the company back. Announcing the new structure, Monsanto's chairman said that he and his colleagues would be subject to "both the upward opportunities and the downside risks inherent in stock ownership." In other words, the scheme ensured that managers share regret with shareholders – and be driven by similar incentives.

In general, then, stock options are an example of a win-win contract. In defiance of conventional finance theory, both parties to the contract are happy because they calculate the risk-adjusted value of the options differently, meaning that they can agree on a price. Financial, business, and commercial, even sporting life, is full of examples of such contracts. Consider the following:

- Swaps. Both sides benefit from these financial transactions, which either convert interest payments from fixed to floating rates (or vice-versa) or one currency into another. In a typical currency swap, for instance, a U.S. firm that can borrow cheaply in its home market converts the money to a foreign currency, say French francs, by swapping it with a French firm that wishes to borrow in dollars. Both firms end up with cheaper funds than they could have raised on their own.
- Catastrophe insurance bonds such as the hurricane bonds described in Chapter 1.
- Credit derivatives. These are new instruments that allow banks to lay off concentrations in their lending caused by accidents of geography. For instance, an American bank might lay off some of its credit risk to its local borrowers in return for taking on some of the credit risk of an Italian bank. The chances that both types of borrowers will default at the same time are obviously much lower than the chance of one set of borrowers running into trouble.

- Michael Jordan's multimillion-dollar contract with the Chicago Bulls (so long as Mr. Jordan goes on shooting hoops better than anyone else).
- Tiger Woods's lucrative endorsement contract with Nike (ditto, but substitute golf balls for hoops).
- Credit card loyalty programs. What the card issuer gives up by way of rewards it gains from increased contact with its customers over time.
- Savings plans offered by telephone companies. As competition has become intense in America and other countries, phone companies have offered consumers a savings bonanza. In one case, for instance, an AT&T customer in New York switched his long-distance business to MCI's 12-cents-a-minute plan, only to be offered $50 to switch back to AT&T's "new" 12-cents-a-minute plan. Despite sharply reduced revenues from calls, AT&T still benefits because it profits from line rentals and other services. Hence its newfound willingness to offer a winning deal to consumers. Many peoples' long-distance bills have fallen by four-fifths in the last two or three years.
- Mutual and co-operative societies. These work when members collectively can do business more efficiently than if they acted as individuals. For instance, a mutually owned mortgage company can use the power of numbers to offer its members cheaper home loans. Hence membership offers a win–win contract.

Where people or firms fail to make proper risk-adjusted calculations, they can still find themselves in win-lose contracts. The most glaring example of a firm that was shot through with such contracts is Britain's Barings Bank. When it collapsed in early 1995, most people drew a single lesson: that a rogue trader had been allowed, through a combination of incompetence and greed, to run up losses that literally broke the bank. Thinking of the episode in terms of upside and downside creates a much more nuanced picture of Barings's downfall. For instance, Nicholas Leeson, the rogue trader in question, had a free option on the upside and very little personal regret until his crimes got out of hand. For him, the operational and trading free-doms he was allowed amounted to a contract in which he stood to gain at the bank's expense. He stood to make big bonuses so long as his trading schemes continued and he was reporting substantial profits to London.

His bosses there were seduced by the impact his profits would have on their own bonuses: they mistakenly saw his profits as resulting from a win–win contract. Thanks to the option-like nature of the bank's bonus schemes, those managers were concerned for their own upside, and thus largely failed to protect the firm as a whole (and its bondholders, who thought their investment was ironclad) from regret. Their implied view was wholeheartedly bullish, which makes it less amazing with hindsight that there was very little interrogation of Leeson's profits before it was too late. Surely for the bank to be making huge profits in Singapore it had to be taking risk or commit-ting fraud. If the bank had adjusted Leeson's performance for those risks it would have formed a very different picture of his behaviour long before he had run up huge losses. In the wake of Leeson's antics, many banks now have a healthy suspicion of unusually strong upside. Even a bank that is bullish and therefore inclined to seek risk is far more likely to question success as well as failure.

Another sad example of a win–lose contract is the experience of Sony Corporation in Hollywood. It signed up leading studio execu-tives with what looked like win–win contracts. It failed to realize, however, that it had in effect handed those executives a blank cheque with which to spend its shareholders' money. When Sony bought into Hollywood it saw mainly the upside of one big box office hit after another. It underplayed the downside risk represented by a string of expensive flops – precisely what happened. But if it had adopted a risk-adjusted stance, it might have structured its contracts more sen-sibly, only rewarding managers if they delivered results and putting clear limits on their ability to spend money. Any firm which hears that one of its subsidiaries has a reputation for lavish spending, espe-cially in an industry which is hard to impress, should pay serious attention. The chances are that it is suffering from a win–lose contract that will cause it regret.

A remarkable Hollywood win-lose contract was Michael Ovitz's infamous $97 million handout in 1997 after a brief nine-month career with Disney. Mr. Ovitz is a talented entertainment executive, but it seems crazy that he or any other individual can ever earn so much money for so little work. The losers on the contract were Disney shareholders, who got little if anything for a large expenditure. In general, where managers are granted so-called "golden egg" clauses in their contracts, it is at shareholders' expense. The managers in question rarely have a deserving case for so much upside, even if they manage to convince a board of directors of the opposite. Indeed, the fact that a potential recruit even asks for a golden egg might be seen as implying a bearish view on his prospects.

Another common win-lose contract is the subject of enormous vexation and remarkable passivity. The parties involved usually know from experience that they are entering into a horribly skewed deal, but they go ahead and do it anyway: they contract to buy a house. The craziest cases can be found in Britain, specifically in England. There, house buyers have amazingly little power, except in one circumstance when they can turn the table on sellers. Assume for a moment that house prices are rising and you wish to buy. A seller asks for £200,000 and you are willing to pay that price. You agree on a deal and shake hands. Under the English system, however, it can take several weeks before formal and legally binding contracts are "exchanged." And in this period a terrible thing can happen. Known as "gazumping," essentially the seller exercises a free option to sell at a higher price to someone else. It is unclear whether the nastiest form of gazumping is where the seller uses the threat to pull out as a means of extracting more money from the original purchaser or where the seller simply pulls out and deals with the new buyer. Either way, the practice causes enormous stress and misunderstanding. The real estate agents who act as intermediaries have little incentive to arbitrate or seek fair play. In the end, their commission will be higher if the final price is higher.

Occasionally, buyers have the same power, but in reverse. When prices are falling and demand for houses is also falling, a buyer might try to drop the price at the last minute by threatening to walk away.

This happened in Britain in the early 1990s and left a generation of bruised homeowners calling for reform of the system. Now that house prices are rising again, however, the bruising is happening all over again, with buyers bearing the marks.

We can see why this system is crazy if we analyse it using upside and regret. In a rising market, the seller has no downside if she uses gazumping to extract a higher price – there is no legal recourse for the maltreated original buyer. In one sense, therefore, it is perfectly rational for the seller to play this cruel game. After all, an extra £10,000 or £20,000 can make a big difference. Only personal morals might stop someone from chasing this upside as hard as they can.

From the buyer's perspective, until contracts have been exchanged and a legal obligation established, the system is inherently unattractive. No business would grant a free option to a supplier or customer equivalent to the option house buyers are forced to grant sellers. In some cases, this option can cost the buyer thousands of additional pounds. At worst, it can break a deal by moving the price beyond the buyer's means. The potential regret is therefore enormous.

Why do people tolerate this system? The situation is bizarre, because almost everyone in England either has first-hand experience of gazumping or has watched friends get hurt by it. One answer is that rising house prices are seen as conferring more net benefit than loss, so politicians have been reluctant to intervene. However, simple changes would remove the option that turns even the most honest sellers into potential deal breakers. In Scotland, for instance, there is no waiting period before a legal contract exists. Pulling out of deals there can involve forfeiting a deposit of up to 10 per cent of the purchase price, something that concentrates the minds and morals of all parties. Indeed, by requiring both sides to make a deposit that can be forfeit, the Scottish system in effect places a premium on the option to walk away. Deals still fall through, of course, for reasons other than greed. In these cases, however, the deposit acts as an insurance premium that protects the other party from harm. Because there is a single price on the option, Scottish buyers and sellers alike are treated the same. This is a win-win system, but one which recognizes that sometimes one party will lose.

England is not alone in its misery. Rising prices in the United States often produce win–lose contracts, simply because demand tends to outstrip supply. In New York, for instance, bad habits became prevalent amidst strong market conditions after mid-1996. Would-be buyers placed offers, often mailing their deposit cheques, only to find that theirs was one of several bids that the seller would keep on the table in case a rival deal fell through and that until then the seller had no intention of cashing their cheque. Horror stories abounded. In many cases the problems can be traced to the lack of a penalty affecting the seller. Although a 10 per cent deposit is normally required from the buyer, the seller, in effect, keeps her free option on the upside.

Britain also offers one of the world's finest examples of a win–lose contract, an example that also powerfully illustrates how better thinking about risk can help us to avoid catastrophe. In 1992, executives at Hoover, a manufacturer of vacuum cleaners, came up with what they thought was a neat marketing ploy. Under pressure from their American parent company to improve sales and profits, Hoover's bosses endorsed a promotion that offered customers an attractive deal: if they spent £100 or more on a new Hoover product, they would earn two free round-trip air tickets to Europe. This proved successful, so much so that Hoover's factory began working around the clock to meet demand. Then, however, the firm's managers made a huge leap: faraway America became the promised destination for would-be purchasers. For the average traveller, such tickets were worth perhaps £400, far more than the value of the underlying product. Not surprisingly, sales of Hoovers more than jumped. Consumers by the thousands quickly realized that their upside from the promotion was worth far more than the downside of buying a new machine that they may not have needed. Meanwhile, those who had thought of replacing an old or tired machine were given a powerful reason to buy a Hoover rather than a rival brand.

Promotions rely on the win–win idea if they are to be successful. The customer thinks she is getting a good deal, while the promoter achieves more sales than would otherwise have been the case. The extra costs for the promoter are thus offset by obvious benefits.

Unfortunately, Hoover had blundered its way into a disastrous win-lose contract with its customers. And it was the loser. As more and more people claimed free air tickets it became clear that the idea had gone much further than Hoover's management had ever anticipated. Rival businesses began to exploit Hoover's embarrassment. One carpet retailer, for instance, cheekily offered would-be customers who spent £999 or more on its carpets a free Hoover – a deal that explicitly carried it with the free air tickets promised by Hoover! As people bought new machines that they did not really need they began to try to sell them for less than they had paid. After all, with air tickets in the bag it scarcely mattered if a consumer "lost" £40 on his £100 purchase – the net result was £400 of air travel for a tenth of the price. A flourishing market in unused Hoover goods sprang up, cannibalizing the very business the promotion was supposed to help.

As the disaster unfolded, Maytag, Hoover's parent company, was forced to intervene. Three Hoover bosses were fired, including the highly paid chief executive. In the end, Maytag had to set aside no less than £48 million to cover the fiasco. It set up a task force that at its peak had 250 staff trying to sort out the mess caused by tens of thousands of claims for tickets. By one estimate, some 100,000 Hoover products were purchased in 1992-93, so the number of tickets at stake was huge. To top the commercial disaster, Hoover found itself with a customer relations nightmare. Thousands of people could not get the flights they expected, often because Hoover cited "small print" that limited availability. Many sued the firm, arguing that the promotion had been misleading. Lawsuits, some of which are still before the courts as we write, have cost Hoover further sums.

How could a company ever have contemplated such a promotion? On the face of it, Hoover never stood to make money on a deal that gave customers much more than they were paying to buy a vacuum cleaner. Indeed, a simple upside-downside analysis would have been sufficient to alert Hoover's managers to their potential problem. But, like those corporate treasurers who bought exotic and risky derivatives because they had a big incentive to make small extra returns, Hoover's managers were under pressure to make the business perform better. Dogged by past losses, when they contemplated the promotion they gave too much weight to the effect on sales and profits of the greater sales volumes that they expected to result from their free offer. Instead of asking what could go wrong, they reached for the upside. By doing so, they and their firm suffered very large regret.

Whenever firms create incentive schemes or seek ways to make parts of their operations do better, they probably expose themselves to hidden risks. Maytag failed to consider that its reasonable pressure might cause risky behaviour by Hoover. Plenty of banks have discovered that traders will do crazy things if they think that their bonus will be made secure by a big payoff. And plenty of firms face risks that they are often unaware of as they try to make sales staff more effective.

As an illustration of this last point, a friend of one of the authors once came home grinning from ear to ear. He had just visited a car dealer hoping to find out the price of a new model of Jeep that he wished to buy as a replacement for his current vehicle. An unusually pleasant salesman had offered him a deal that was simply too good to refuse: if he signed that day he could trade in his old car for the new one, in effect buying the new model at a bargain price. Bowled over, he signed. And, unlike most such deals, this one turned out to be the genuine thing – the shining Jeep was acquired almost for nothing.

Was this mere luck? Had he come across a salesman who was leaving that day and wanted to harm his employer? Well, it turned out that luck was involved. But the salesman had no ill will towards his firm. Rather, he was working under an incentive scheme that occasionally gave him an urgent need to sell one more car. The day our friend turned up was the final day in a period of three months during which the salesman would earn a big bonus for meeting a predefined target. He was one vehicle away from meeting the target. He therefore had so much to gain from that one sale that he did not care if he virtually gave the car away – which is almost what he did.

If the deal was a win-win contract for the salesman and our friend, it was certainly not a good thing for the car dealer as a whole. The dealer "lost" the profit it would otherwise have made from a customer who was inherently likely to trade up at some point in future.

A better incentive scheme might have established a more sophisticated target – for instance, the number of cars sold weighted by the average margin at which they were sold. This would have the effect of keeping employees' desire for upside in balance with the firm's need for profits.

It always pays to ask whether we might inadvertently have given someone a motive to act in ways that are against our interests. The Jeep salesman's boss needed to rethink an otherwise sound compensation plan. How many managers should examine schemes that supposedly give staff incentives but in reality lead to bad decisions? Think back to our earlier analysis of mutual funds and we can suggest that a structural problem in that industry is that fund managers have incentives that lead to bad decisions on behalf of investors.

This point reminds us of the idea of implied views. Sometimes we will encounter situations where it is obvious that our counterparty is desperate to do a deal with us, even if the deal looks suspiciously cheap. Perhaps the deal is genuinely win–win. It is more likely, however, that some perverse incentive is causing our counterparty to offer terms that would be crazy from another perspective. In such cases, there is a danger that underneath the surface lurks a win–lose contract. But provided we think the contract will be honoured (and this can be a big risk!), then we have little to lose by signing. Of course, we had better be sure that the "lose" element of the contract is not in fact attached to us!

The simple terms we have introduced for describing risk have broad applications when they are combined into a common language. They work with precision in technical situations when we must weigh two clear alternatives that offer specific payoffs for specific risks. But they also work as a framework for shaping how we think about less precise decisions in life and business. For the upside we are being offered, what is the downside in the context of our appetite for risk? Does this deal or decision make sense on a risk-adjusted basis, so that we can be confident we are entering a win–win contract? Have we thought of scenarios under which our apparently win–win contract could turn out to be win–lose?

In sum, it seems reasonable to suggest that people should enter into deals only if they perceive the result to be win-win on a risk-adjusted basis. Each person's risk-adjusted value will depend on:

1. The scenarios they are considering, which determine the calculation of upside and regret.
2. Their degree of risk aversion (lambda), which is context-dependent.

In negotiating a deal, one can affect the risk-adjusted value of one's counterparty by altering their perceived scenario set, by biasing it either up or down. Alternatively, one can alter the payoffs. In the end, the art of deal-making is to find the minimum payoffs that will give one's counterparty a positive risk-adjusted value and make them sign.

9

MAKING GOOD THINGS BETTER

Once we begin to manage risk, it is as if we accept a responsibility to ourselves, either personally or corporately. At a simple level, this means trying to think about decisions in ways that capture more of the nuances of everyday life. Using upside and regret, we can bring some rigour to our approach to even the most intractable of dilemmas.

But the responsibility we assume goes deeper than this. We can quite correctly couch many of our risk questions in terms of "Should I buy this or that?" But if we are to be true risk managers then it also follows that we should ask, "How can I remake what I have today in order to realize the best risk-adjusted returns in future?" This captures the reality that we always have a starting position when we make a decision. Even if, to use the example that opened Chapter 5, we gain a $5,000 windfall, our starting point for deciding what to do with the money is that we now have $5,000 in addition to our existing assets and liabilities. Typically, we do not hold that money in isolation.

The logic of trying to improve what we have today is a powerful one. Later in this chapter we will suggest some societal implications, but let's concentrate first on what it means for individuals. Thanks to the difficulty of measuring performance and the propaganda of the mutual funds industry, it is tricky for most people to gain an overall view of their portfolios. It is even harder for most of us to quantify in any way our overall financial health; simply to consolidate all the relevant information would be beyond most people's ability.

Imagine, however, that we could see a picture of our net wealth that showed its risk-adjusted characteristics and how they matched our lifelong investment needs. Our first reaction might be shock. No doubt thousands of us would be horrified to realize that we hold some quite inappropriate assets. Thousands of others might see for the first time that they have systematically mismanaged their wealth. If we are really to have sensible portfolios then we have to understand how the different elements interact with each other. This is known as covariance and is a central idea in modern finance.

Viewing our wealth in this new way we might quickly realize something else: that by changing the elements of, or adding new elements to, the portfolio, we could tweak our picture so that it better matched our ideal image as the best risk-adjusted portfolio for our needs and risk appetite.

This is also one of the central ideas in modern finance. Harry Markowitz, whose work on portfolio theory won him a Nobel prize and the just tag as the father of modern finance, was among the first people to realize the intimate linkages between risk and reward. Among his insights was to see that any portfolio can be compared to an optimal portfolio that is perfectly balanced between risk and reward. To earn a certain level of return we must accept a commensurate level of risk. However, it is possible to take more risk than is necessary to earn the same return. Thus, there is what is known as the "efficient frontier" – simply, a line that describes risk-efficient portfolios. A goal of professional finance is to construct "optimal" portfolios that are as close as possible to the efficient frontier.

We can see enormous potential gains from better risk management using upside and regret. If a single person optimizes her portfolio, then the gains are small and narrow. But if thousands or even millions do it, then the gains are huge and widespread. People would suffer fewer disastrous financial shocks, which would mean less need for the big government bailouts that are required by today's accidents. And a lot more of people's wealth might be freed for productive use.

Imagine the same approach applied to the banking system. If one bank optimizes its portfolio, it might find that it needs less operating capital for the same book of business. A bank with $5 billion of capital could free, say, $50 million of capital while still operating with sufficient cushion to reassure regulators that it is not a threat to the banking system. Capital that is not available now would be freed up.

If banks optimized en masse, the overall effect on an economy would be huge. And because the gains come from money that is tied up at present, there would be no adverse impact on inflation. Banks would simply be making better use of what they have.

The same applies to businesses of all kinds. If firms were able to allocate capital just slightly more efficiently than they do today, the effect on the competitiveness of business would be dramatic.

How does optimization work?

Any given portfolio has a mark-to-future that has both upside and regret (downside). The essence of investing successfully is to strike an appropriate balance between the two. Any investment decision entails a trade-off between the potential for increased upside and the risk that the downside will be unacceptably high. Add more upside and your regret will grow. Just where do you draw the line?

This is where mathematical optimization comes into play. The goal of every investor should be neither to maximize returns nor to minimize risk. It should be the maximization of risk-adjusted returns in a forward-looking framework. As long as the investor is looking backward, there is no risk, so risk-adjusted returns have no meaning. In a mark-to-future paradigm, the investor should maximize the risk-adjusted return which we have defined to be the upside minus the cost of insuring the downside. Fortunately, this is relatively easy to do.

The concept of the optimized portfolio – one that has been adjusted for risk to achieve the greatest efficiency – can have far-reaching consequences. Think again of the banking system. The benefits from optimizing would not just derive from the banks' ability to allocate capital more efficiently. If they optimized their loan portfolios on a risk-adjusted basis, then they should become more stable: they would be less vulnerable to unexpected shocks from lots of loans going sour at the same time. This would dampen the volatility of the banking system and make the economy better able to withstand any changes in the environment.

Before too long computer technology will deliver software programs that also will allow ordinary people to gain a much clearer picture of their assets and liabilities. The signs of such developments are already abundant, though few such programs have been released commercially. Several big financial firms are working on programs that will guide users through otherwise impossibly complicated investment calculations. The capacity of such programs to simplify procedures and to educate users should not be underestimated. In 1997 one small band of software rebels launched CapScape, a program designed to allow people to bypass banks when they try to raise capital for their businesses. This is not the same as giving investment advice, it is true. But the program has cut the time required for creating a flotation's documentation from 900 hours to less than 20. And by obviating the need for expensive intermediaries, it makes the capital-raising process more efficient as well as faster. Programs such as this will have more and more impact as they emerge from code-writers' cubicles.

There are other ways in which individuals will be able to benefit from portfolio optimization. Financial firms – brokers, insurers, and banks – will increasingly work with their customers to rationalize their financial assets. This may seem a strange assertion. Surely brokers are famous more for churning their clients' accounts than for giving sensible risk-adjusted advice. Surely insurers are better at mis-selling investments and policies than at leading customers to well-rounded portfolios. As for banks, haven't they traditionally been bad at everything? True enough. But think of how financial services is changing as an industry and a different logic emerges.

Until perhaps a decade ago, different types of financial firms operated largely in isolation from one another. There were some grey areas. Merrill Lynch invented a brokerage account that looked much like a chequing account. But mostly insurers competed with each other, banks competed with banks, and brokers with brokers.

Things have changed. Even while we were writing this book, dozens of mergers were announced around the world that cut across once-rigid industry lines. Now banks vie with brokers and insurers to sell an array of similar investment and insurance products. Although there are some remaining regulations that limit competition, these cause more nuisance than real disruption.

As financial services increasingly become a single industry, the optimizing effect will tend to kick in. When you were merely a broker, you sourced product (shares and bonds) and you tried to sell them to customers in return for a fat commission. When you only sold insurance, you shamelessly steered customers towards policies that gave you the best commissions – you didn't really care if you were condemning them to earn lousy returns.

Often, consumers themselves assist in their own exploitation. Peter Carroll, a consultant with Oliver, Wyman & Company in New York, likes to point out that several groups of customers generate significant earnings for financial service providers despite the existence of more attractive alternative services:

- Home-owning credit card customers who maintain a balance and pay non-tax-deductible interest.
- Purchasers of mutual funds that charge up-front commissions.
- Buyers of many forms of life insurance.
- People who leave large balances in non-interest-bearing current accounts.
- People who "tuck a traveller's cheque in their drawer for a rainy day."

With the barriers between different branches of the industry breaking down, however, the same firms that once made merry have acquired a peculiar obligation to do the right thing by their customers. They still stand to benefit by selling more products and services to their customers – indeed, arguably such cross-selling should be highly cost-effective. The firm should also benefit if it can deepen its relationship with customers, who will then be less likely to leave. But – and here's the rub – for each successive service offered to an existing customer, the greater is the value of the existing service relationships which are being put at risk by the sale of a potentially inappropriate product. So firms will increasingly find it is in their interest to do the right thing and help their customers to optimize their finances. As Mr. Carroll says, "The emerging obligation for these firms appears to be *to do what is right for each customer*, rather than simply to maximize sales. This obligation will – on some level – be a 'moral' or 'ethical' one. In future, it could easily come to be codified as a 'legal' one."

Of course, there is no accounting for everyone's tastes. For some people, the peace of mind represented by $200 worth of traveller's cheques mouldering in a desk drawer more than compensates for the lost interest on their money. For others, the 18.9 per cent interest paid on a credit card balance, though not tax deductible, may be less psychologically onerous than feeling that their home could be forfeit under a home equity line of credit. Perhaps buying a high-cost mutual fund through a known investment advisor is the equivalent of using a personal shopper at Prada to choose a dress instead of shopping at Sears or The Bay. However, in time there will be more and more pressure on the firms that sell these products to change their habits. They will be increasingly reluctant to sell things that are patently not "right" for the majority of their customers. And this should create a powerful trend towards optimization.

That is the good news. The bad news is that we should not hold our breath in readiness for a helter-skelter rush towards some financial and economic nirvana. As with past changes in finance, it is the big institutions that will reap the early benefits as well as take the early risks. It will be many years before we routinely expect optimal advice from intermediaries and can require optimal decision-making of ourselves. But the trend is clear. And it is based on all of the building blocks we have outlined in this book.

Everywhere we look, we can find social and business arrangements that could be improved using a better risk-management framework.

Formal optimizing is mostly the stuff of high finance, but we can suggest some ways in which the idea of optimization might help.

Since the 1980s there have been big changes in the rules that govern banks. Successive banking crises led to international efforts to make banks put aside capital when they lend money or trade in markets. The 1988 Basle Accord and similar agreements set such rules for lending and much breath was expended in the negotiations that produced them. Subsequent rules are gradually coming into force for the price risks that we described in Chapter 8.

Some of these rules are stupid. The lending rules, for example, require banks to put aside capital equivalent to 8 per cent of a loan they make to a corporation. It does not matter whether the corporation is a globally respected and financially solid giant or a struggling minnow; the capital charge is the same. Daft, no? Banks therefore have no capital incentive to lend sensibly (though of course they have other incentives!). Similarly, the price risk rules are riddled with problems, many of them to do with how the overall riskiness of a bank's activities should be measured.

By now, we hope we have shown that the problem of measuring risk of any kind is complicated. There is often more than one solution. In future, however, our risk-management framework could be used to change the very basis of regulation for financial institutions. We suggest that financial firms of all kinds be required by a central authority (such as a central bank or financial regulator) to account daily for the amount of regret in their portfolio under certain ordained scenarios. (Alternatively, and more liberally, firms would have to show the scenarios they had used in calculating their regret.) The regret number would then form the basis of a centralized insurance scheme. The regulator would sell each firm an option that protects it against its regret, ensuring on a daily basis that there is no scope for failure. The premiums charged for the options would generate a central risk fund that could be used to compensate firms that suffer unexpected extreme negative outcomes, thereby conferring much greater stability on the financial system. This system would, in effect, create a risk tax that would protect society against the ill effects of an unlucky or a consistently poorly managed firm. It would also act as an early-warning system because a firm that begins to take lots of risk would attract higher and higher option premiums, much as an over-exposed trader often faces growing margin calls. This could stop a rogue firm before it does much damage to anyone except itself. At the same time, however, the system would not discourage risk-taking behaviour. It would rather ensure that this is undertaken in a more considered fashion because institutions would have to buy insurance rather than rely purely on self-insurance.

Such a system would go a long way towards more optimal regulation. The rules would exist not for their own sake, but in order to protect against extreme losses. And they would encourage better behaviour by the individual constituents of the market, thereby promoting greater efficiency. Of course, we will not see such a system soon, but the related ideas of regret, benchmarks, and optimization create a powerful tool kit with which the system can be rebuilt.[*]

---

[*] The interested reader can obtain more information about optimization from R.S. Dembo, "Optimal Portfolio Replication," Algorithmics Research Publications, available on the internet from www.algorithmics.com.

10

KNOW YOUR RISK

S cott Adams, creator of the cartoon character Dilbert, came up with an intriguing idea: creating the perfect food. Here is how Mr. Adams described the idea according to an article in *The New York Times*. Imagine you could create a burrito that was entirely healthy. People who ate the burritos would feel better and would want to eat more of them. As word spread, more people might think more about their health and eat a little better, even if that only meant munching a healthy burrito instead of a fat-laden one. But let's be optimistic. Suppose the idea really caught on and that, as a result, the health of Americans improved by a little as 5 per cent. The consequent reduction in health care and medical costs would be massive – billions of dollars would be freed for people to improve their standard of living. As Mr. Adams says, "I love anything that has no downside and potential gigantic upside."

It is not strictly true to say that Scott Adams's perfect food idea has no downside: some investment would be required and it would take a big marketing effort to popularize the "Dilbert burrito." But on a risk-adjusted basis, the upside from his scheme makes it hugely appealing. In this it is similar to programs designed to prevent disease. The cost of vaccination is much smaller than the cost of treating someone who has become sick. It is worth noting, too, that Mr. Adams also implicitly understands the idea of optimization: in this case, a small improvement in everyone's health can create disproportionately large benefits. Perhaps Mr. Adams should consider writing the "Dilbert Guide to Investing in Mutual Funds"!

Throughout this book we have seen examples of ways in which people are struggling to find a language that allows a systematic and reasoned approach to risk, but which does not abandon the intuitions and fears that we feel in our gut. Whether for Alan Greenspan or Scott Adams, we hope that we have gone a long way towards codifying such a language. And from that language, we can derive a simple set of rules which, taken together, should offer a beginning for better risk management.

We would not like to create the impression that we are offering a risk panacea for anyone careful enough to make a few calculations. As we have said, risk is an extremely subtle and complex idea, full of fascinating byways and confusing cul-de-sacs. It defies easy capture. But we owe it to ourselves to make the attempt. Whether we are politicians, business leaders, investors, or just plain individuals, we can all do better if we seek to take control of risk.

Our starting point is simply to observe that risk is the result of the uncertainty we face in the future. Useful measures of risk should therefore look forward, not backwards, in time. To the extent that history plays a role in risk measures, it is in defining reasonable scenarios for future events. Mostly, our future follows smoothly from our past. One day follows from the next with only incremental changes in the environment. Thus, in all but totally chaotic systems, the past can be a guide to the future. But we must use such guidance with great care. The further ahead we look, the larger will be the likely deviations from past events. Occasionally there is a shock to the system: a market crash, an earthquake, a pyramid scheme that runs out of control, etc. Risk management is about being able to deal with both typical and unusual events.

By definition, unusual events are difficult to predict using information derived exclusively from the past. Proper measures of risk should account for both typical and atypical situations. But how far should we go? Should we consider the possibility of the stock market going to zero value? Should we assume that it is possible for three earthquakes a day to hit Tokyo for the next ten days? Where do we draw the line between atypical and unbelievable? A framework for risk measurement must be able to accommodate an enormous diversity of opinions about the future; no one person can have the imagination or experience to foresee every eventuality. It must be able to deal with the past as a guide to the typical. It must include subjective assessments of the sort that we make all the time. It must be general enough to be able to handle a multitude of risks. And it must be able to present many different measures of risk, each of which might be suitable for different situations.

To define such a framework we need a definition of financial risk; *Financial risk is a measure of the potential changes in value that will be experienced in a portfolio as a result of differences in the environment between now and some future point in time.*

An essential prerequisite to risk measurement is our ability to determine the value of our present position. If we are unable to value our holdings today, then we are unable to measure the change from today's value that the future could bring under our chosen scenarios. As a consequence, we will be unable to measure our risk. This determining of present value is known as "marking our position to market."

Rule 1: Know the value of your holdings today.

Since the risk we assume will depend on how far in the future we wish to look, choosing the horizon over which risk is to be measured is essential in order to compute a value for risk. Different situations lead to different time horizons. For example, a pension plan manager has a need to control risks over much longer periods than a trader.

When we think about our individual financial goals, we may have a series of objectives over time that will determine how far ahead we look at any given moment. For instance, while we are saving for our retirement in a decade's time, we might also need to buy a new car tomorrow.

Rule 2: Pick an appropriate future time horizon.

Risk will depend on the possible events we describe for tomorrow. These should accommodate many types of forecasts: estimates based on history, subjective estimates, and estimates based on models. Probably the most general way to describe risk is to use scenarios. Each scenario leads to a future value for the portfolio under consideration. The appropriate collection of scenarios captures the likely variation in the parameters that could occur between now and the time horizon we have chosen. As we have seen, scenarios are extremely general in nature and, if they are aptly chosen, can capture all the richness we need.

Omitting important possible events will lead to poor risk measures. Placing too heavy an emphasis on extremes may also lead to erroneous conclusions. That is why choosing scenarios is akin to the art of risk management. There are many mechanical techniques that will guide the choice of scenarios. These methods are usually good at generating the more typical events. There is a fine line between extreme, atypical situations that have value in decisions made today and events that could not conceivably occur. It is the proper choice of extreme scenarios that separates artists from technicians. This leads us to the third rule of risk measurement.

Rule 3: Choose a wide range of scenarios to describe possible future events. Include extremes and scenarios that contradict popular opinion. Include scenarios with negative outcomes that would cause regret. Assign a likelihood to each scenario.

At the very least, once scenarios have been chosen and the horizon has been determined, we will need to value our holdings under each scenario at the horizon. This will give a range of possible values that the portfolio might assume in future.

In most situations, risk is not an absolute measure. It is invariably the risk of one action versus some other action. Put another way, it is the risk of one portfolio as compared with some other portfolio. For example, the risk might have to do with buying a stock versus keeping your portfolio unchanged. It is important in such a case to measure the risk not only of holding the stock alone but also of holding the stock plus the original portfolio versus holding the original portfolio. In this case the original portfolio is the benchmark. This is important because the future of the original portfolio as well as the single stock will depend on the chosen scenario. The incremental risk of holding the stock in addition to your portfolio will be different from the risk of holding the stock alone.

You can always compute the absolute risk of a portfolio by making the benchmark null (that is, setting it to zero). This brings us to the fourth rule of risk measurement:

Rule 4: Pick a benchmark.

We are now in a position to quantify risk. And here is the really amazing thing about our approach to risk: once our scenarios and benchmarks have been determined, all that is left are calculations that are mechanical in nature. We have done what we can to reduce uncertainty as far as is humanly possible.

Rule 5: Value your portfolio and benchmark at the horizon under each and every future scenario.

We refer to this as marking-to-future. Marking-to-market results in a unique number because there is no uncertainty in the number – it is today's value. Marking-to-future results in an array of possible numbers, one for each uncertain event at that point in the future.

Now, clearly we can choose whatever risk measure we like. One of our central points about risk is that it means different things to different people and institutions. Different measures are applicable to the many consumers of financial risk information. A fund manager might be wholly unmoved by statistics that would be extremely useful to a bank regulator. Yet one remarkable aspect of risk measurement is that the raw numbers that go into these different risk measures are always the same! They are always obtained from a valuation of your portfolio and benchmark under all scenarios. The measures come in many disguises, but at the end of the day they are all derived after Rule 5 is applied, either implicitly or explicitly.

Our risk-measurement framework can be applied with many different risk measures. But the one that is appropriate is always context-dependent. This leads to the sixth rule of risk measurement.

Rule 6: Compute the appropriate risk measure based on values obtained by applying Rule 5.

In this framework all risk measures are computed from the same underlying information – the values of the portfolio and benchmark at the horizon under all possible scenarios. The risk measures themselves become simply different statistics computed on the calculated data. For example, a value-at-risk number is one such statistical measure (and one that we have argued should be used with care). The standard deviation, or volatility as it is sometimes called, is another. Regret is a third. Best-case and worst-case measures generally ignore the tiny probabilities involved, but they are still simple statistics at the extreme points on the distribution of outcomes. Without doubt, other new measures that are relevant to specific categories of investors or institutions will appear in future.

The measure we prefer, since we believe it most accurately captures the true cost of risk, is regret. Regret is simply the absolute loss relative to the chosen benchmark under each scenario. It is positive when, if the scenario in question were to occur, you would regret having invested in your portfolio. To measure regret:

1. Compute the difference in the horizon values between the portfolio and the benchmark under each scenario.

2. Regret is zero whenever this number is positive – we should feel happy about our portfolio in this case.
3. Regret is the absolute value of the difference whenever this value is negative.
4. Average regret is the probability-weighted sum of the regrets under each scenario.

As we have seen, there are many useful ways of applying regret. First, we have argued that regret is exactly what an insurer would have to pay you if he insured the downside on your portfolio relative to the benchmark. To see this, notice that the insurer pays nothing if you outperform the benchmark and pays the absolute value of the difference if you underperform the benchmark. Thus the true value of this regret is the price you would have to pay for such insurance today. We can foresee that insurance in future might explicitly provide protection against regret, something that could change financial markets in fundamental ways.

Since regret, properly priced as insurance, is exactly the cost of eliminating all downside risk with respect to a benchmark, and since the benchmark can be arbitrary, regret can properly be used as a comparative measure, which is not the case for other risk measures such as VaR. For the value of regret you can eliminate risk entirely. Regret is therefore an appropriate measure for allocating your capital among businesses (or, if you are an individual, allocating your money between investments). We regard regret as a "perfect" measure of risk.

The importance of our risk rules is that they separate the process of risk management into distinct and logical steps. The choice of scenarios is separate from the choice of methodology for valuation, which is in turn separate from the particular choice of risk measure. By understanding this, it is easy to compare risk measures. It is also easy to know when a particular risk measure is relevant.

As we have seen, combining regret with upside and then factoring in our appetite for risk using a measure such as lambda creates a powerful new way of approaching decisions. In many instances we will make better decisions because we will think more clearly about the array of outcomes that could happen in future. We can use scenarios to describe that array. And, as we have seen, simply by adopting the right benchmark we can change the way we think about many problems.

We will never eliminate regret. It is in the nature of things that bad, occasionally terrible, events happen that change our lives forever. Managers do make bad bets that ruin their careers. We might buy too much of an investment that collapses and ruins us. Plenty of us get our fingers burned in the housing market because we put too little weight on regret.

But we can use regret against itself. If we know our potential regret, we can avoid situations in which we are exposed. Or we can minimize our regret by insuring against it. Where there are efficient markets, we can do this relatively cheaply. But sometimes we will pay whatever it takes to obtain peace of mind, to the extent that we might walk away from a deal entirely. It is this impulse that must dominate our thinking about risk.

AFTERWORD

In late 1994 one of the authors made a disastrous decision that has caused him immense regret. Over the stated objections of his wife and the scepticism of other family members, he sold their house just outside of London, England, intending to avoid the property market while he was posted abroad in New York for a few years.

With what he thought was impeccable logic, he analysed the decision as follows. House prices had stabilized after a steep decline in the early 1990s and showed no sign of upward movement. The British economy was growing slowly but unspectacularly. At best, house prices might be stable, but there was, the author believed, no chance that they would rise sharply. People had absorbed the lessons of the 1980s bubble and were unlikely to chase prices much higher. Equally, there seemed little prospect of a sharp fall in prices, given that houses had not even returned to the levels seen during the late 1980s. Moreover, because the rent he could obtain on the house was less than the mortgage payments required to keep it, there would be a short-term cost that would be difficult to justify while living in an expensive city such as New York. Better to sell the house and place the small amount of equity from it in a fixed-rate account. The house was duly (and quickly) sold.

During 1995 and the first half of 1996 there was little reason to regret this decision – house prices were indeed going nowhere fast. Thereafter, however, the market took off with a vengeance. As middle-class families chased houses in the catchment areas of good state schools, they exposed a limited supply of large houses and a dearth of sellers in the town in question. Families in London discovered the town as a pleasant place to live and a tolerable commute. They created a new category of demand and, crucially one with plenty of ready cash on hand to bid up prices.

Prices rose in leaps and bounds. By late 1997, a house that was previously valued at, say, £100,000 would comfortably have fetched £170,000, a whopping increase that would have been pure equity had the author only owned it! Indeed, the family's original equity stake would have quadrupled had the house sold for around that price. By this stage, the regret caused by the original decision to sell had become enormous. Indeed, the "loss" of that equity had become the factor that constrained his family from buying back into the market. Prices had simply run too far ahead of his ability to pay.

It is easy to be wise after the event. Indeed, there is a certain psychological pain attached to that hindsight wisdom. After eighteen months, it did not seem that a big mistake had been made. A year further on and the picture had entirely changed.

What really strikes the author now, however, is how a bad decision might have been avoided by better analysis. The ideas in this book could have provided the tools.

For instance, what time horizon did the author use? When making the original decision, he fixed on the immediate months after moving abroad and gave much weight to the negative impact of the small monthly payments that would be necessary to fund the house in Britain in the event that it was rented to tenants. But arguably the correct time horizon was several years hence when he and his family might return to Britain and need to live in a house once again. That would be the point at which they might benefit from having been continually exposed to the market because they would have fared as well or as badly as everyone else. There would be no inherent disadvantage.

Second, the author was guilty of dreadful scenario planning. He dismissed the idea that prices might rise sharply, and he thereby failed to consider what missing out on a big rise might mean. He focused instead on the single forecast that house prices would be largely unchanged, something that proved utterly wrong in reality. Like Paul Reichmann in Mexico, he unknowingly made a huge gamble while believing that he was in fact being sensible.

This combination of an incorrect time horizon and a single scenario were fatal. But the author might still have avoided disaster had he understood the idea of regret. Indeed, he might have overcome the two other failings because regret alone would have helped him to think through the issue better.

In this case, his real regret came not from a short-term cost, but rather from the long-term deficit caused by being out of the market. The loss of the equity he would have made had he only kept the house meant that he could not afford to re-enter the market at the same level or higher, a regret that was massive by comparison. Just weigh it up. It would have cost, say, £250 each month to keep the house. Over three years, then, the author's maximum downside was £9,000 plus any decline in house prices. But the upside (which the author did not even grace with a tiny probability, choosing instead to ignore it!) was potentially huge. In the event, it was more than seven times the potential downside. As his wife now ruefully exclaims, where else in life can one earn this much simply by sitting tight?

Unwittingly, then, the author in question has learned the hard way that bad financial decisions can cause enormous regret. His only consolation is that he now has a way to think through problems that should help him to minimize future regret. Other people facing similar dilemmas might take the same comfort from the ideas and rules suggested in this book.

INDEX